Prophet
of
Justice

UNDERSTANDING THE BOOK OF AMOS

William J. Doorly

Paulist Press/New York/Mahwah, N.J.

To Elba de la Caridad Santamarina Doorly
whose life-enhancing support makes things happen

Acknowledgments
Paulist Press gratefully acknowledges the use of excerpts reprinted by permission from *Amos Among the Prophets* by Robert Coote, copyright © 1981
by Fortress Press; excerpts reprinted by permission from *Joel and Amos* by
Hans Walter Wolff, copyright © 1981 by Fortress Press; excerpts reprinted by
permission from *Tribes of Yahweh* by Gottwald, published by Orbis Books;
excerpts reprinted by permission from *Amos, A Commentary* by James Luther
Mays, published by Westminster Press.

Library of Congress Cataloging-in-Publication Data

Doorly, William J., 1913-
    Prophet of justice : understanding the book of Amos / by William
J. Doorly.
       p.   cm.
    ISBM 0-8091-3089-0 : $5.95 (est.)
    1. Bible. O.T. Amos--Criticism, interpretation, etc.   I. Title.
BS1585.2.D66   1989   89-8741
224'.806--dc20   CIP

Published by Paulist Press
997 Macarthur Boulevard
Mahwah, NJ 07430

Printed and bound in the
United States of America

Contents

Preface

I would like to thank several friends who assisted me in my effort to understand the relevance for today's world of the Old Testament scriptures. These include Ethel Fairchild, Frank Stephens, the Rev. Donna Day-Lower, my neighbor, A. Joseph Berger, the Rev. Ronald Lutz, Pastor of the Church of the Brethren, Ambler, Pa., and Dr. Foster R. Mc Curley, former St. John Professor of Old Testament at the Philadelphia Lutheran Theological Seminary. These all stayed with me through several years of independent study.

I would also like to thank Dr. David Hopkins, Old Testament Professor at the Wesley Theological Seminary, Washington, D.C. for his fine book *The Highlands of Canaan*, and for the many discussions we had together. I owe a special thanks to Jorge Troncoso my fellow worker at CORA Services for teaching me how to use the Macintosh Computer to produce the charts of the divisions of the Book of Amos which appear in this book.

I would like to thank my wife, Elba, to whom I dedicate this book, whose support and encouragement are essential ingredients of my efforts.

Finally, I would thank J. Michael Schell, James Harron and the administrative staff of CORA Services along with The Sisters of the Good Shepherd in Philadelphia for the logistical support which they provided.

Scriptural references in this work are from the Revised Standard Version unless otherwise noted.

Introduction

When Bible students, and Bible readers in general, arrive at the prophets they usually find the going tough. The story line disappears and in its place the reader encounters strange phrases, unfamiliar expressions and sudden, unexpected, twists and turns. The effect is not usually soothing and is often jarring to the reader. There is a real value, however, in moving forward in this rough terrain. If we want to become familiar with life in those ancient times in that part of the world, and I assume that this is a worthy goal, the prophetic books will help us.

Scholars have identified more than twenty forms of prophetic speech. (These include such forms as laments, dirges, announcements of judgment, reports of visions, intercessions, etc.) These forms of speech developed naturally, and if we try to imagine speech patterns as being related to the geographical areas where they emerge (which is a plausible theory), then the writings of the prophets may assist us in becoming familiar with the terrain of ancient Israel.

One of the chief characteristics of the land of ancient Israel, the highlands of Canaan, is the geomorphological *diversity* of the entire area.

What this means in simple terms is this. If you found yourself in any location in the highlands, you could travel in any direction and witness changes in the environment, including such things as vegetation, soil content, rock composition, altitude, slope. What we are looking at, writes David Hopkins in his book on Israelite agriculture, *The Highlands of Canaan*, is "... an exceedingly complex canvas" and a "fractured topography."[1] The one thing constant to travel in this area is discontinuity. I am sure you get a similar feeling as you work your way through some of the prophetic books. In a real way, if we are serious in our studies, we can look on the rough surface as an assist in understanding the ancient authors we are studying. We shouldn't want it any other way.

We are conditioned to take prophecy in small doses. The use of the prophets by the New Testament writers encourages us to use this approach. And there are undoubtedly some students who approach the study of the prophets like someone rooting through a box, rearranging the shredded packing paper and the excelsior in search for a jewel or some other valuable item. This, I am sure, is how some preachers use the prophetic books. They search for a text on which they can build a sermon.

Approaching the prophets in this way will not lead to an understanding of the person, or persons, behind the book. Moreover, there are themes developed throughout the books which can only be comprehended when we are able to stay with the author for a period of time. It also helps to understand the political and economic events which are taking place at the time of writing, the "situation of life," and for this we will need the assistance of scholars. But we are not without this assistance. There are many fine books available for our use if we are willing to put forth the effort.

In this book I will attempt to show how the hypothesis of three layers of authorship for the book of Amos will enable us to get a firm grip on the teachings of several Old Testament theological perspectives, and how these perspectives move us in the direction of understanding the Old Testament as a whole.

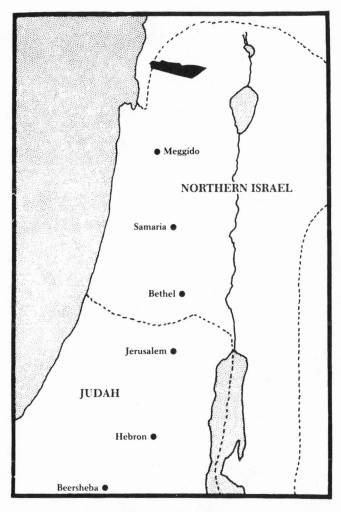

In the seventh century edition of the book of Amos, Tekoa was identified as the home of Amos. Tekoa was a small village in the highlands south of Jerusalem. From Tekoa, looking to the east, the Dead Sea could be seen eighteen miles away and three thousand feet below.

Amos lived in Judah, but prophesied in the northern kingdom of Israel.

CHAPTER I

How Some Scholars Have Divided the Book of Amos

Amos of Tekoa prophesied in the middle of the eighth century. Along with Micah of Moresheth, and Isaiah of Jerusalem, Amos was primarily a preacher, not a writer. It is possible that these prophets wrote nothing. The oracles which they delivered were written down by persons who wanted to record their words because they considered them valuable and worth preserving. We sometimes call these recorders, or scribes, disciples of the particular prophet whose oracles they recorded, but in reality we know very little about them, and the word disciple may or may not be appropriate.[1]

Before the oracles of the eighth century prophets reached their final form, as they appear in our scriptures, subsequent authors and editors wrote additional material including introductions, conclusions, editorial comments, liturgical insertions, and third person narratives.

In our movement toward understanding books written in ancient times we encounter some obstacles. Books written in ancient Israel were not written the way books are written today. Most books of the Bible had more than one author. Even if a book had one primary author, an editor or a redactor made subsequent additions before the book reached its final form. In order to understand the book of Amos we have to become familiar with its layers of authorship. Ideal knowledge would involve knowing who said it (or wrote it), when it was written, and for what purpose. To assist us in this sorting out of the book of Amos and to become familiar with the problem of identifying the words of the eighth century prophet

(and distinguishing them from the additions of later authors/
editors who did not live in the eighth century) we are going to
examine the work of three current scholars who have produced books on Amos. As you read this chapter, if you are not
familiar with the book of Amos, some of it will not be com-
prehensible. There are two ways to proceed here. One way is
to have your Bible handy and read the sections identified (by
chapter and verse). The other is to press forward, picking up
as much as possible, with the intention of rereading the chapter later when you are more familiar with the book of Amos.
At any rate, this chapter is very basic, and I can't think of a
better place to put it than where it is.

The three books which we will review for the purpose of
deciding how to divide the book of Amos are *Amos, A Commentary*, part of the Westminster Press series "Old Testament
Library," by James Luther Mays;[2] the Amos portion of H.W.
Wolff's commentary *Joel and Amos*, of the Fortress Press
"Hermeneia" series;[3] an essay on the book of Amos published
by Fortress Press entitled *Amos Among the Prophets* by Robert B. Coote.[4]

Amos, A Commentary by James Luther Mays

Like Gerhard Von Rad, and many others, Mays starts his
book with the assumption that *most* of the book of Amos is
based on the prophecies of Amos of Tekoa who preached in
the days of Jeroboam II. He writes, "The larger part of the
material can be attributed with confidence to Amos."[5] He then
identifies portions of Amos which he *does not* attribute to the
original prophet. These are:

(a) Deuteronomic additions: these include the three oracles
to Tyre, Edom, and Judah (found in chapters 1 and 2), the dat-
ing in 1:1 (the words ". . . in the days of Uzziah king of Judah
and in the days of Jeroboam the son of Joash, king of Israel"),
and the theory of prophecy in 3:7 which reads

> Surely the Lord God does nothing without revealing
> his secret to his servants the prophets.

(b) Hymnic poetry: 1:2, 4:13; 5:8f; 9:5f; and possibly 8:8.
Mays says that these came from a cultic source in Judah.

> The LORD roars from Zion,
> And utters his voice from Jerusalem;
> The pastures of the shepherds mourn,
> And the top of Carmel withers (1:2).

> For lo, he who forms the mountains, and creates the
>   wind,
> And declares to man what is his thought,
> Who makes the morning darkness, and treads on the
>   heights of the earth,
> The LORD, the God of hosts, is his name (4:13).

> He who made the Pleiades and Orion and turns deep
>   darkness into the morning, and darkens the day into
>   night,
> Who calls for the waters of the sea, and pours them out
>   upon the surface of the earth,
> The LORD is his name (5:8).

> The LORD God of hosts, he who touches the earth and it
>   melts, and all who dwell in it mourn . . .
> Who calls for the waters of the sea, and pours them out
>   upon the surface of the earth—
> The LORD is his name (9:5–6).

(In chapter III, "The Seventh Century Scribe of Jerusalem,"
we will suggest the purpose of these hymnic insertions.)

(c) **Disciples:** they provided the third person narrative concerning Amos and Amaziah, the priest of Bethel.

(d) **Exilic or post-exilic:** this comprises the oracle of salvation found at the end of the book, 9:11–15.

(e) **Fragments:** these include the divine title "God of Hosts," scattered explanations such as the time spent in the wilderness (2:10 and 5:25), and the identification of the deities in 5:26.

Division of the Book of Amos as presented by James L. Mays in *Amos, A Commentary*

1	2	3	4	5	6	7	8	9
V.1 Title	Against Moab 1 – 3	1 – 6 Exodus Wisdom series,	1 – 3 Cows of Bashen	1 – 7 Fallen is Israel	1 – 7 Woe to those who are at ease	1 – 9 First three visions	1 – 3 4th vision	1 – 4 5th vision
V.2 Hymnic Material	Against Judah 4 – 5		4 – 5 Bethel	8 – 9 Hymnic Material			4 – 7 You trample on the needy	5 – 6 Hymnic Material
Against Damascus 3 – 5	Against Israel	7 Prophets		10 – 12 Trample on the poor	8 – 10 Pride of Jacob			7 – 10 I brought Israel from Egypt
Against Gaza 6 – 8	6b – 8 You sell the righteous	8 – 12 Witness Samaria's destruction	6 – 11 Five former judgements	13 – 15 Wisdom Literature	11 Great house smitten	10 – 17 Amaziah at Bethel	8 Hymnic Material	
Against Tyre 9 – 10	9 – 12 Destroyed the Amorite		12 Prepare to meet God	16 – 20 Wailing	12 – 14 Do horses run on rocks?		9 – 10 Day to be darkened	
Against Edom 11 – 12	13 – 16 The cart	13 – 15 Bethel to be punished	13 Hymnic material	21 – 25 I hate your feasts			11 – 14 Famine of God's word	11 – 15 The Booth of David
Against Ammon 13 – 15								

Words of Amos ☐

Later Additions ▨

Mays wrote his commentary in 1969. In his preface, he states that he ". . . can only regret not having had the opportunity to see more than one fascicle of Wolff's commentary on Amos in the *Biblischer Kommentar*."[6] It is our fortune, however, to have the English translation of Wolff's commentary.

Joel and Amos by Hans Walter Wolff

The English translation of Wolff's commentary on Amos was published by the Fortress Press in 1977 as part of the Hermeneia series. It is the most comprehensive commentary on the book of Amos to date. In the foreword Frank Moore Cross, Jr. asserts that the Hermeneia series ". . . will utilize the full range of philological and historical tools, including textual criticism . . . the methods of history tradition (including genre and prosodic analysis), and the history of religion."[7] Wolff's commentary is for everyone, for scholars as well as the rest of us.

Wolff divides the book of Amos into twenty-three sections or pericopes. For every division in the book of Amos Wolff provides comment under four headings: Form, Setting, Interpretation, Aim. This procedure works well, assisting the reader to keep in touch with the three important questions: Who said it? When did they say it? What was their point?

Brackets are used in the English translation to indicate segments of text which Wolff considers to be later interpolations. For example:

> The words of Amos [who was among the sheep breeders,] from Tekoa which he viewed concerning Israel [in the days of Uzziah king of Judah and in the days of Jeroboam the son of Joash, king of Israel,] two years before the earthquake (1:1).

If we remove the brackets, we see the verse in an earlier version according to Wolff's judgment.

> The words of Amos from Tekoa which he viewed concerning Israel, two years before the earthquake.

For every one of the twenty-three divisions of Amos, Wolff
provides a separate bibliography; and before the pericope gets
the four part treatment (Form, Setting, Interpretation, Aim),
Wolff examines every word or expression in the original language and compares divergent manuscript readings. To
ensure that nothing is left out, Wolff adds generous footnotes.
The first pericope of Amos, consisting of only two verses (1:1–
2), has ninety footnotes.

As a result of his atomistic approach to the text of the book
of Amos, Wolff identifies *six layers of authorship* as follows:[8]

A. "The Words of Amos of Tekoa"

The preaching of the original prophet from Tekoa, and the
earliest form of the book of Amos, is found basically in chapters 3 to 6. Wolff refers to this section as the teaching of an
itinerant prophet from Judah who may have wandered
between Samaria and Bethel.

B. The Literary Fixation of the Cycles

This layer includes five of the eight oracles against the
nations (Damascus, Gaza, Ammonites, Moab, and Israel), and
the visions which begin in 7:1. Wolff surmises that the two
groupings were fixed literarily at the same time.

C. The Old School of Amos

This school of Amos had "... at its disposal remembered
deeds and sayings of the prophet which were transmitted as
part of neither the 'words of Amos from Tekoa' nor the
recorded cycles."[9] The school was active in Judah from 760 to
730 B.C.E. It was responsible for the narrative concerning
Amaziah the priest of Bethel (7:9–17); the references to Isaac
and Beersheba; words of woe in 8:9–10 and 13–14 where Yahweh says, "I will turn your feasts into mourning and all your
songs into lamentation"; the reference to the remnant of
Joseph in 5:15 and the ambiguous word "perhaps"; and the
past tense in 6:6 where the hearers "are not grieved over the

ruin of Joseph." The old school of Amos ". . . brings relation-ships of substance to light."[10]

D. The Bethel-Exposition of the Josianic Age

In 2 Kings 23 King Josiah, as part of his program to unite the people of Israel (those who remained in the north and those of Judah) and centralize control of Yahwism, is reported to have completely destroyed and defiled the altar at Bethel, a competitive cult center. The D historian includes in his early history of the northern kingdom a story of a prophet from Judah (probably based on a tradition of Amos) who spoke out against the altar in Bethel, predicting that a descendant of the house of David, Josiah by name, would tear apart the altar. Wolff writes: "In the days of Josiah . . . the book of Amos was searched so thoroughly for references to Bethel, or even merely to an 'altar,' that no passage was overlooked which lent itself to interpretation in light of Josiah's action."[11] The only genuine reference to Bethel by Amos was in 5:5 (Bethel shall come to adversity) which Wolff considers the trigger for the additions to Amos in the days of Josiah. To this source also belongs the hymnic material in 4:13; 5:8f; and 9:5f, and also possibly 1:2, "Yahweh roars from Zion and raises his voice out of Jersualem." Elaborations by this author ". . . are merely attached to the catchwords 'Bethel' and 'altar.'"[12]

E. The Deuteronomistic Redaction

Here is the origin of the three late oracles against the nations, Tyre, Edom, and Judah (according to Wolff). The pur-pose was to bring to Judah the benefit of the warnings of Amos. Here we find references to the prophets (2:10–12, and 3:7, "Surely the Lord does nothing without revealing his secret to his servants the prophets"). The prediction concern-ing the coming day of hunger for the word of Yahweh, 8:11–12, may not have originated with D but with the old school of Amos. D is responsible for the extension of 1:1 to synchronize the activity of Amos with Jeroboam II and to associate him with the sheep breeders.

F. The Post-Exilic Eschatology of Salvation

A post-exilic theologian "... adds, briefly but distinctly, that Yahweh's sentence of death is not his last word" (9:11–15).[13]

Amos Among the Prophets by Robert B. Coote

The author of this book calls it an essay. It differs from the two works above in that it does not systematically work its way through the book of Amos, but instead divides the text into three sources based on a broad hypothesis developed by the author. In presenting this hypothesis the author states that he is oversimplifying, but he explains frankly why and how in a manner which is convincing and reassuring. Coote's approach to Amos is summed up in his words:

> ... scholars are now coming to understand that almost every prophetic book is instead a complex tapestry of strands from different tradition sources, perhaps more like the current picture of the composition of the Pentateuch than anything else.[14]

Coote's theory states that the book of Amos consists of three major sections written in the eighth century, seventh century, and sixth century respectively. He calls the three sections Amos A, Amos B, and Amos C.

A. Amos A[15]

Amos A consists of the preaching of the prophet from Tekoa. We do not know whether Amos wrote any part of his oracles, or whether someone else did, but the style is oral. He is specific and poetic, and he delivered his message of doom to Samaria in the third quarter of the eighth century. There are nine distinctive features of the A-stage oracles, including: (1) they are addressed to a specific class in a specific time and place, (2) they all contribute to a "*single basic message*,"[16] (3) they were delivered orally, and (4) they announce inevitable catastrophe.

We do not know the original sequence of the A-stage oracles because the B-stage editor/author may have rearranged them, but in their present arrangement, the preaching of Amos begins in chapter 2, verse 6, as part of the oracle against Israel, with the words:

> Thus says the LORD:
> Because they sell the righteous for silver
> And the needy for a pair of shoes—

A-stage oracles continue to be scattered through every chapter except chapter 7. They end in chapter 9 with these words:

> And though they hide from my sight on the bottom of
>   the sea
> There I will command the serpent, and it shall bite
>   them.
> And though they go into captivity before their enemies,
> There I will command the sword, and it shall slay them
>   (9:3–4).

The A-stage oracles become more identifiable when you become familiar with stage B. Coote says after you become familiar with the B-stage and C-stage characteristics, the A-stage characteristics ". . . will grab you by the collar."[17]

B. Amos B[18]

The B-stage author was a writer, not a preacher, whom Coote describes as a scribe of Jerusalem in the last days of the seventh century after the death of Josiah and before the destruction of Jerusalem. Coote writes, but only after fifty-six pages of convincing argument:

> The B stage, then, was composed in Jerusalem late in
> the seventh century by a scribal adjunct to the ruling
> elite; through writing and the art of literature, he
> expresses and preserves on behalf of the ruling elite

the desire to maintain the status and power of Jerusalem as a sociopolitical center, and the motivation to
put this power to use in a program of customary and
judicial reform.[19]

Whereas the eighth century prophet dealt only with
Samaria, the B-stage author deals only with Bethel. Characteristics of the B stage author include the following: he
addresses a general audience (Amos addressed the elite of
Samaria); it shows signs of being a written composition; it is
not specific as Amos was, but uses vague words like "good"
and "evil"; and "... in contrast to the A stage, the B stage
offers *an open future, a new possibility.*"[20]

In the A stage, punishment was coming because of oppression of the poor; in the B stage punishment is more often
linked to the rejection of the prophets' message. All passages
in Amos concerning prophets and their rejection are B stage
passages including the narrative concerning the priest of
Bethel, Amaziah.

Also, the B stage editor has a fascination with the number
5. He has five oracles against the Nations (Aram, Philistia,
Ammonites, Moab, Israel), five groups of oracles against
Bethel, and five visions. In Chapter 4 there are five former
punishments or judgments sent by Yahweh which end with
the words "... yet you did not return to me." These five end
with the *therefore* which introduces the words "Prepare to
meet your God."

An interesting point is made by Coote in conjunction with
the fact that the B stage shows the signs of being a written
composition. Before the publication of his commentary, Wolff
published a book called *Amos the Prophet*[21] in which he compares the speech patterns of wisdom literature with the
speech patterns of Amos and concludes that Tekoa was a center of rural wisdom tradition, from which Amos came. Coote
points out that none of the characteristics of the wisdom tradition come from the oracles of Amos, the 8th century
prophet, but can be attributed to the B stage author, the 7th
century scribe.

C. Amos C[22]

This stage was written in the last third of the sixth century, after the final destruction of Jersualem and the final exile of its ruling class. On the other side of the captivity, the B-stage composition needed updating. The beginning and the ending were edited. The three oracles against the nations, Tyre, Edom, and Jerusalem, were added. And a new ending was added (9:7–15), including the oracle of salvation.

It is not the throne of David which will be restored, or the kingdom of David, but the *hut* or *booth* of David. Coote writes:

> The reference is to the early David, the folk hero, the protector of the disenfranchised, the David of the byways and caves of the Judean hill country, sprung from the country town of Bethlehem, the ruler who knew his subordination to Yahweh, and who delayed the building of the temple that would serve in folk memory as the functional symbol of despotic royal power.[23]

Summary of the Above Views

Let us compare the three views concerning the authorship of the book of Amos reviewed above. All three authors agree that the three late oracles against the nations (Edom, Tyre, and Judah) are not based on the words of Amos, the eighth century prophet. There is also agreement that the oracle of salvation at the end of the book (9:11–15) was not based on the words of Amos. The question must be raised whether any of the oracles against the nations are based on the words of Amos. All three agree that the core of the oracle against Israel is based on the words of Amos, beginning with the words "Because they sell the righteous for silver." Coote states that the introductory numeric phrase borrowed from wisdom tradition, "For three transgressions of . . . and for four . . ." was not the language of Amos of Tekoa. He argues that except for the core of the oracle against Israel, none of the oracles against the nations is based on Amos A. Robert Wilson in his book

Division of the Book of Amos as presented by Robert B. Coote in *Amos Among the Prophets*.

1	2	3	4	5	6	7	8	9
v.1 Title	Against Moab 1 - 3	1 - 8 Exodus	1 - 3 Cows of Bashan	1 - 2 Fallen is Israel	1 - 7 Woe to those who are at ease	1 - 17 First three visions	1 - 3 4th vision	1 - 4a 5th vision
v.2 Hymnic Material	Against Judah 4 - 5	Wisdom series, Prophets	4 - 5 Bethel	3 - 7 Seek me and live	8 - 10 Pride of Jacob		4 - 7 You trample on the needy	4b - 6 The earth melts and rises
Against Damascus 3 - 5	Against Israel	9 - 12 Witness Samaria's destruction	6 - 11 Five former Judgements	8 - 10 Pleides and Orion	11 Great house smitten	Amaziah at Bethel	8 Like the Nile	7 - 15 I brought Israel from Egypt
Against Gaza 6 - 8	6b - 8 You sell the righteous	13 - 15 Bethel to be punished	12 Prepare to meet God	11 - 12 Trample on the poor	12 - 14 Do horses run on rocks?		9 - 10 Day to be darkened	(Booth of David)
Against Tyre 9 - 10	9 - 12 Destroyed the Amorite		13 Hymnic material	13 - 15 Seek God			11 - 14 Famine of God's word	
Against Edom 11 - 12	13 - 16 The cart			16 - 20 Wailing				
Against Ammon 13 - 15				21 - 25 I hate your feasts				

AMOS A 8th Century

AMOS B 7th Century

AMOS C 6th Century

Prophecy and Society in Ancient Israel states that "oracles against foreign nations seem to have been a function of central Jerusalemite prophets."[24] This being the case, it would point to the origin of these oracles as other than Amos A unless we are willing to identify Amos as a central Jerusalemite prophet.

All three authors ascribe the narrative of Amos and Amaziah, the priest of Bethel, to someone other than Amos himself. Coote points out that this story promotes and bolsters the Deuteronomic belief that the destruction of Israel was related to Israel's rejection of Yahweh's prophets (2 Kgs 17:13–14 and 21–23), rather than Samaria's treatment of the poor.

In constructing Amos B, Coote blends together at least three of Wolff's six layers of authorship, (1) the literary fixation of the cycles, (2) the Bethel-exposition of the Josianic age, and (3) the Deuteronomic redaction. Coote also subtracts from chapters 3 through 6 (the part of the book of Amos identified basically by Wolff as based on the words of Amos of Tekoa) five Bethel oriented passages which he identifies as belonging to Amos B (see 3:13–15; 4:4–13; 5:14–15; 5:21–27; and 6:8–14). Coote states that Amos A only preached at Samaria, and that in the late seventh century Amos B elaborated on the Amos of Tekoa sayings to include Bethel.

For the remainder of this book we are going to work with the three-layers-of-authorship model of Robert Coote. This is my choice for pragmatic reasons; it works and it is neat (compact). Coote calls his approach an oversimplification, and it will be in our best interests if we keep in mind that the scribe of Jerusalem (Amos B) may have been more than one person, possibly a school which reflected the needs and viewpoints of Jerusalem in the days of King Josiah. But before we get to the Deuteronomic scribe of Jerusalem we have to become familiar with the original oracles of Amos of Tekoa.

CHAPTER II

Amos, the Eighth Century Prophet of Tekoa

The eighth century prophets are the first biblical characters without a veil of myth and legend. Hosea, Amos, Isaiah, and Micah perform no miracles, and, apart from some Isaiah narrative, do not play a key role in the nation's history. They are not presented as deliverers of the people, nor are they pictured as being in positions of great importance in the nation's history. Their place in the history of Israel—and they occupy an important, strategic position—is determined by the words which they spoke and the ideas which they presented in their oracles—in other words, their preaching.

While it is not possible to determine "without a shadow of a doubt" the exact words of Amos, the original prophet of Tekoa, I am convinced that we can accept the hypothesis of Coote that the oracles of Amos are found positioned in a framework provided by a seventh century author whose Deuteronomic theology was more intricate than the theology of the original preacher.

Accepting this hypothesis as reasonable, we will reproduce here from the Revised Standard Version the probable words of the eighth century prophet.

> Because they sell the righteous for silver, and the needy
>   for a pair of shoes—
> they that trample the head of the poor into the dust of
>   the earth, and turn aside the way of the afflicted;
> a man and his father go in to the same maiden, so that
>   my holy name is profaned;

they lay themselves down beside every altar upon
    garments taken in pledge;
and in the house of their God they drink the wine of
    those who have been fined.

"Behold, I will press you down in your place, as a cart
    full of sheaves presses down.
Flight shall perish from the swift, and the strong shall
    not retain his strength, nor shall the mighty save his
    life;
he who handles the bow shall not stand, and he who is
    swift of foot shall not save himself, nor shall he who
    rides the horse save his life;
and he who is stout of heart among the mighty shall flee
    away naked in that day," says the LORD.

Proclaim to the strongholds in Assyria, and to the
    strongholds in the land of Egypt,
and say, "Assemble yourselves upon the mountains of
    Samaria,
and see the great tumults within her, and the oppression
    in her midst."
"They do not know how to do right," says the LORD,
    "those who store up violence and robbery in their
    strongholds."
Therefore thus says the Lord God:
"An adversary shall surround the land.
    and bring down your defenses from you,
    and your strongholds shall be plundered."

Thus says the LORD: "As a shepherd rescues from the
    mouth of the lion two legs, or a piece of an ear, so
    shall the people of Israel who dwell in Samaria be
    rescued, with the corner of a couch and part of a
    bed."
"Hear this word, you cows of Bashan, who are in the
    mountain of Samaria, who oppress the poor, who

crush the needy, who say to their husbands, 'Bring,
    that we may drink!'
The Lord God has sworn by his holiness that, behold the
    days are coming upon you
when they shall take you away with hooks, even the last
    of you with fishhooks,
and you shall go out through the breaches, every one
    straight before her;
and you shall be cast forth into Harmon," says the LORD.

Hear this word which I take up over you in lamentation,
    O house of Israel:
"Fallen, no more to rise,
  is the virgin Israel;
forsaken on her land,
    with none to raise her up."

Because you trample upon the poor and take from him
    exactions of wheat,
you have built houses of hewn stone, but you shall not
    dwell in them;
you have planted pleasant vineyards, but you shall not
    drink their wine,
you who afflict the righteous, who take a bribe, and turn
    aside the needy in the gate.

Therefore thus says the Lord,
"In all the squares there shall be wailing; and in all the
    streets they shall say, 'Alas! Alas!'
They shall call the farmers to mourning and to wailing
    those who are skilled in lamentation,
and in all vineyards there shall be wailing, for I will
    pass through the midst of you."

Woe to you who desire the day of the LORD! Why would
    you have the day of the LORD?
It is darkness and not light; as if a man fled from a lion,
    and a bear met him;

or went into a house and leaned his hand against the
     wall, and a serpent bit him.
Is not the day of the LORD darkness, and not light, and
     gloom with no brightness in it?

"Woe to those who are at ease in [original word missing]
     and to those who feel secure on the mountain of
     Samaria,
the notable men of the first of the nations, to whom the
     house of Israel come!
Pass over to Cahneh, and see; and thence go to Hamath
     the great; then go down to Gath of the Philistines.
Are they better than these kingdoms? Or is their
     territory greater than your territory,
O you who put far away the evil day, and bring near the
     seat of violence?

"Woe to those who lie upon beds of ivory, and stretch
     themselves upon their couches,
and eat lambs from the flock, and calves from the midst
     of the stall;
who sing idle songs to the sound of the harp, and invent
     for themselves instruments of music;
who drink wine in bowls, and anoint themselves with
     the finest of oils, but are not grieved over the ruin of
     Joseph!
Therefore they shall now be the first of those to go into
     exile, and the revelry of those who stretch
     themselves shall pass away."

For behold, the LORD commands, and the great house
     shall be smitten into fragments, and the little house
     into bits.

Hear this, you who trample upon the needy, and bring
     the poor of the land to an end, saying, "When will
     the new moon be over, that we may sell grain?

And the sabbath, that we may offer wheat for sale,
that we may make the ephah small and the shekel great,
    and deal deceitfully with false balances,
that we may buy the poor for silver and the needy for a
    pair of sandals, and sell the refuse of the wheat?"

The Lord has sworn by the pride of Jacob:
    "Surely I will never forget any of their deeds."

"And on that day," says the Lord God,
    "I will make the sun go down at noon,
    and darken the earth in broad daylight.
I will turn your feasts into mourning,
    and all your songs into lamentation;
I will bring sackcloth upon all loins,
    and baldness on every head;
I will make it like the mourning for an only son,
    and the end of it like a bitter day."

"Smite the capitals until the thresholds shake,
    and shatter them on the heads of all the people;
and what are left of them I will slay with the sword;
    not one of them shall flee away,
    not one of them shall escape.

"Though they dig into Sheol, from there my hand shall
    take them;
though they climb up to heaven, from there I will bring
    them down.
Though they hide themselves on the top of Carmel, from
    there I will search out and take them;
and though they hide from my sight at the bottom of the
    sea, there I will command the serpent, and it shall
    bite them.
And though they go into captivity before their enemies,
    there I will command the sword, and it shall slay
    them."

Who Was Amos?

Tradition tells us that Amos lived in a small town twelve miles south of Jerusalem named Tekoa. From Tekoa you could see the Dead Sea, eighteen miles away and three thousand feet below. In Tekoa, and in the other small towns throughout the rural areas, Amos could see the suffering of the families of Judah and Israel. He saw their poverty increasing and their hope disappearing as the limited resources of this relatively poor country were used to support the monarchy, the king's army, the courts of the land, and even the priests and prophets of the shrines. Yes, even the priests and the prophets either did nothing to relieve the hardships of rural life, or, even worse, devised ways to profit from the defenselessness and vulnerability of the poor.

One day, somewhere in the wilderness south of Jerusalem, the God of Israel came to Amos while he was "following the flock" and made him a prophet. At the right time Amos left the town of Tekoa, trudged across the Judean desert past the city of Jerusalem on his left, crossed the northern border of Judah, bypassed the city of Bethel, and arrived in the busy, prosperous capital city of the northern kingdom, Samaria. There he delivered his oracles.

To Whom Amos Spoke

If we look at the words which Coote identifies as the words of Amos A, the eighth century prophet, we identify those to whom he spoke as the strong and the mighty (2:14), ". . . the people of Israel who dwell in Samaria" (3:12), "House of Israel" (5:1), and "Those who are at ease in [original word missing] and . . . those who feel secure on the mountain of Samaria." These are those who have profited materially from the changes which took place in Israel when the monarchy was established with its need for a capital city and centralized power. Along the way they have become greedy and have severed themselves from the values of old Israel. They can be called the elite of Samaria. They have become rich at the expense of others. They have clustered themselves around the monarchy but are not necessarily members of the royal court. These are the people of power and privilege.

The Sins of Those Addressed by Amos

(a) Some constitute a merchant class, whom Amos says cannot wait until the sabbath is over so they can continue to cheat the poor with false balances and sell ". . . the refuse of the wheat."
(b) They are involved in the administration of justice, ". . . who take a bribe and turn aside the needy in the gate."
(c) They are the wives of the rich who place demands on their husbands, influencing them to ". . . crush the needy" (4:1).
(d) Some have profited from the present structure of society to such an extent that they can only be described as greedy, idle, and self indulgent. They ". . . stretch themselves upon their couches, and eat lambs from the flock . . . sing idle songs . . . drink wine in bowls, and anoint themselves with the finest oils" (6:4–6).
(e) Amos says of these that they ". . . do not know how to do right . . . those who store up violence and robbery in their strongholds" (3:10). They have built houses of hewn stone. Some have more than one house. They have used ivory (imported from Africa) to decorate their houses and their beds.
(f) By their behavior they ". . . trample the head of the poor into the dust of the earth."

Those Who Were the Victims

The people who are oppressed are identified as the poor, as the needy, and in two places as the righteous (2:6 and 5:12). They are the ones who have suffered from the changes in society which the monarchy produced. However long the institutions of pre-monarchical Israel, the shevet (translated tribe), the beth-av, (inter-generational family) and the mishpaha (coalition of inter-generational families) had lasted, by the middle of the eighth century they had broken down in function. Families had lost their land. The old laws concerning the passing of the land through the male line had been ignored. They had become tenant farmers on land which formerly belonged to their families and are now being charged excessive rents. Farmers were pressured to grow, not what they needed for survival, but what the powerful of Samaria needed for international trade. Two of the chief products for trade included oil and wine; these products were far removed from the crops of old Israel when subsistence farming was the way of life. A new justice system, now out of the hands of rural elders and controlled by the urban rich, denied them justice in the gate. In place of the satisfaction of justice they received the bitterness of "wormwood."

What Amos Did Not Say

It is necessary to look at what Amos did not say as well as what he said.

(a) He did not analyze the reasons behind the societal imbalances of his age.
(b) He did not blame the monarchy or the centralization of power for the practices which he condemns.
(c) He did not urge the farmers to organize and overthrow the government.
(d) He presented no program for change and had no solutions.
(e) He did not accuse the people of worshiping other gods or bowing down to idols.
(f) He did not say how good it would be if they could turn back the clock, and return to the "good old days."
(g) He made no reference to a covenant.
(h) He made no reference to a salvation history. All references to exodus, wilderness, and possessing the land were the additions of the scribe of Jerusalem.
(i) He made no references to Yahweh as creator. Phrases like

"... he who forms the mountains, and creates the wind"
are from Amos B.

(j) He offered no hope for Israel, or even for a remnant.

What Amos Said

By looking at what Amos did not say, as we did above, we
prepare ourselves for the narrow platform on which the oracles of Amos are built. As far as we know, no prophet had
appeared previously with such a complete message of doom.
Amos comes with a message of sure destruction for the elite
of Samaria. They have oppressed the poor in the past, and
continue to cheat the peasants of Israel, whom Amos calls the
"righteous." Even the courts have been used to support the
powerful of Samaria in oppressing the farmers.

Yahweh has sent Amos with a single purpose message of
certain destruction. He says:

> Therefore because you trample upon the poor and take
>   from him exactions of wheat,
> You have built houses of hewn stone, but you shall not
>   dwell in them;
> You have planted pleasant vineyards, but you shall not
>   drink their wine ...
> You who afflict the righteous, who take a bribe, and turn
>   aside the needy in the gate.
> Therefore thus says Yahweh, In all the squares there
>   shall be wailing ... and in all the vineyards there
>   shall be wailing, for I will pass through the midst of
>   you, says the Lord (5:11–17).

Amos calls for witnesses to gather on the mountains to see
this destruction which will take place on the day of Yahweh.
He ends his oracles by declaring that not one single oppressor
shall escape.

Although Amos is only concerned with delivering the
words of Yahweh concerning the coming judgment on the
elite of Samaria, the rich and the powerful, for the grossly

unfair treatment of the masses of Israel, there may be a positive side to his message. He was proclaiming that *there was one who did not forget justice.*[1] The God of Amos was after all a God of fair treatment who would not tolerate the abuse of his people.

Where Amos Got His Advanced Ideas About Religion

The hypothesis that the formative years of Israel's origin were the two hundred years preceding the establishment of the monarchy, and that during this time Israel was a coalition of somewhat equal groups living in a contiguous area with no centralized power or authority, explains how the eighth century prophets developed their viewpoint. They got their advanced ideas from the past. They were reacting to the loss of a lifestyle which had previously been characteristic of all Israel. It was from the position of this reaction that Amos declared Yahweh's wrath concerning the exploitation of the masses of Israelites by a small powerful urban class which had developed around the institution of the monarchy.

We cannot be sure that life in old Israel was without incidents of power grabbing and oppression which may have been exhibited in examples of unfair treatment of one group by another. There is always a tendency to idealize the past. I do believe that the interrelatedness of the pre-monarchical institutions and the way they worked to assist the agricultural highland society to survive without central control was a form of proto-democracy. I owe this concept to Norman Gottwald's powerful book, *The Tribes of Yahweh.*[2]

The Survival of the Old Values

This question is sure to be raised, however. Was it possible to preserve pre-monarchical values in the rural areas of Israel and Judah two hundred and fifty years after the end of the federation? One important piece of data suggests a yes answer. After the death of Solomon (900 B.C.E.) elders of Israel would not accept Rehoboam as king because he refused to lighten the burdens of his father's monarchy. Although abuses mirroring those of Solomon developed in the northern kingdom, they obviously took time. The establishment of the northern kingdom must have raised hopes for many that a fairer, more balanced society would result and the values of the past would be maintained. But greed, unleashed from the constraints of the agricultural institutions of old Israel, which stressed the ultimate importance of the *beth-av* and the value of the *mishpaha* in preserving the *beth-av*, along with the rise of an urban class which was able to survive with little or no connection with subsistence farming in a highland environment, began to take its toll. The new structure of society in Israel promoted widespread exploitation of the masses by the royalty and the urbanized rich in both kingdoms.

The Place of Religious Ritual

In the original oracles of Amos there is almost no mention of religious ritual. His only reference to religion is in these words from Yahweh: "I will turn your feasts into mourning, and all your songs into lamentation" (8:10). A hundred years later, Amos B, writing in Jerusalem against the practice of worship in Bethel, penned the powerful oracle found in 5:21–24.

> I hate, I despise your feasts
>   and I take no delight in your solemn assemblies
> Even though you offer me your burnt offerings and
>   cereal offerings,
>   I will not accept them.
> And the peace offerings of your fatted beasts
>   I will not look upon.
> Take away from me the noise of your songs;
>   to the melody of your harps I will not listen.
> But let justice roll down like waters,
>   and righteousness like an ever-flowing stream.

Coote points out a difference in viewpoint between the

Amos A passage (8:10) and the Amos B passage (5:21–24). In the first cited passage Yahweh takes the action (I will turn your feasts into mourning), but in the second cited passage the hearers are urged to take action (Take away from me the noise of your songs). In making this distinction we should keep in mind that any part of Amos B could have been based on words from Amos A, whose identifiable A characteristics have been forever altered by the scribe of Jerusalem. There is one way in which both of these passages agree. Amos A and Amos B agree that Yahweh is not bound or in any way controlled by the rituals of his people. This is what we call the freedom of Yahweh. Performed ritual does not control him. In the theology of Amos Yahweh is a completely free agent. If ritual controlled Yahweh, magic would be operative in Israel's religion. Gerhard Von Rad writes:

> Neither was this Yahweh made available by being influenced by magic; nor could people ward him off by means of magical invocations; nor was it possible, by, as it were, a highhanded drawing upon his powers, to achieve effects which did not proceed in the most direct and personal fashion from himself.[3]

The Relationship Between Amos and Other Eighth Century Prophets

Three of the four eighth century prophets deliver similar oracles referring to the gap between the rich and the poor, and the economic imbalances of their society. The three, Amos, Isaiah, and Micah, are from Judah. Since Amos prophesied exclusively in Israel (the northern kingdom) the words of his prophecy came true first when Israel fell in 722 B.C.E.

It would be intriguing to know if Amos inspired or influenced the other two prophets in the formation of their oracles. In order to compare the oracles of Amos with the oracles of Isaiah and Micah, we would first have to go through the process of reconstructing the books of Micah and Isaiah (chapters

1–39) in the same way that we have reconstructed the book of Amos in our previous chapter.

This would be the starting point. With the information which we now have at our disposal it would be difficult to determine without doubt the role which Amos played in influencing the other two prophets. Perhaps the science of form criticism will improve to the point where comparison of various texts will provide clues as to which came first, or which portion influenced other portions of text. Traditionally, Amos has been recognized as the first of the social prophets. It may be that in addition to the three Judean prophets, there were many others who expressed similar feelings and expressed similar concerns regarding social injustice, but whose oracles never made it to a written document which has survived.

Conclusion

Considering the widespread similarity of the social problems in Israel and Judah, it is my opinion that Amos was one of many, rather than a creative genius. It would be highly unlikely that only three people in ancient Israel felt strongly about the unfairness which existed in the eighth century, and that all three would have prophetic books based on their oracles which made it to the Hebrew Bible in some form. However when the words of Amos are identified and isolated, it is obvious that he was a poet. Reading the book as it now stands dilutes and interrupts the passion and intensity of his message. For example, theological statements from the perspective of a Deuteronomist, or from Jerusalemite wisdom tradition, statements like "Seek good and not evil, that you may live," and "Surely the Lord does nothing, without revealing his secret to his servants the prophets," are completely without passion, and alien to the spirit of the prophet of Tekoa. Later, in Chapter VII we will look at the spiritual implications for today of Amos' preaching.

The oracles of Amos became a written scroll, but they may never have become part of the Bible were it not for the initiative of a scribe who lived one hundred years later. This scribe wanted the people of Jerusalem to hear the message of Amos, the eighth century prophet. Who was this seventh century scribe who placed the oracles of Amos throughout his own literary structure, and what was his purpose?

Before answering these questions and moving to a review of the second step in the development of the book of Amos, there are some social issues with which we should become familiar.

CHAPTER III

A Sociological Detour

You don't have to be a sociologist to understand the economic conditions in rural Israel in the eighth century which provided the ground from which the content and substance of the oracles of Amos of Tekoa grew. However, since valuable background information is available to us in recent studies,[1] I believe that it is in our best interests to summarize some of this economic data. We will do this before turning our attention to the seventh century edition of the book of Amos.

All societies consist of institutions (family structure, government machinery, educational procedures, markets, legal processes, religious organization, theological concepts, etc.). The institutions of a society are functional, that is to say, they function to meet the needs of the members of the society, allowing the society to survive and perpetuate itself.

When the structure of a society is changed, for whatever reason, the institutions are affected in several ways. Let us look at an example of this. The family best suited for an agricultural society is the extended or intergenerational family of three or four generations. The members of this "extended" family live together in one location. There is a role for all members of the family in farming activity, from the young to the very old. (Farming is a very labor intensive activity.) The young assist in the field and can shepherd a flock of sheep as David is reported to have done as a child. The very old can assist with food storage and food preparation.

In pre-monarchical Israel the intergenerational family (*beth-av*) was the central institution. Each family (*beth-av*, literally "house of the father") was allied with other neighboring families (*bete-av*, plural of *beth-av*) for activities beneficial

32

to each individual family, activities which made survival for each family a greater reality. The name of the cluster or alliance of families was the mishpaha. Within the mishpaha there was a very practical sharing of responsibilities, risks, and resources. If necessary there was also a sharing of the fruits of harvest. Here are some of the ways that the families (bete-av) related to and cooperated with each other within the mishpaha.

(a) If a family was attacked by roving bands, nomads, marauders, or mercenary groups hired by the Canaanite city-states located in the plains, members of neighboring families would come to the aid of the attacked family. If the entire mishpaha (alliance of families) was threatened, the neighboring mishpahoth (plural for mishpaha) would come to the aid of the threatened mishpaha. There was no centralized power and consequently no professional army or "state" military institution.

(b) Families within the mishpaha would scatter planting time and thereby make it possible for a larger number of able-bodied persons to participate in ground preparation, planting, cultivating and harvest activity. It was too risky for a single family without a cooperative arrangement with other families to survive. Rain coming too early or too late, or not at all, would eliminate an entire crop. By a cooperative arrangement with other bete-av, the risk of crop failure was spread among the families. Complete crop failure was less likely to be a reality.

(c) There were large facilities which would be too expensive and too labor consuming for one family which could be shared by several or many. These included such things as cisterns, terraces, threshing floors, and storage buildings. The combined labor pool of the mishpaha would make the building and repair of these facilities possible. Non-agricultural projects would include well digging and defense works.

It would not have been possible for the thousands of families which made up the nation called Israel to have survived in the highlands for the two hundred year period before the monarchy without the development of strong functional institutions such as those described here. The highlands provided for the Israelites a less than ideal agricultural environment, but with strong cooperative and interactive social contracts or understandings it was possible to survive.

For families largely depending on subsistence farming to survive, interconnectedness was the absolute rule. The chief beneficiary of the pre-monarchical Israelite social structure was the *beth-av*. It was at the center of a constellation of social institutions. All social forces were positioned to support it. In return the *beth-av* provided for the future of the entire culture by bringing forth children and instilling them with the virtues and values of the agricultural, highland community. This was accomplished by free-will participation and mutual consent without central control. With the arrival of the monarchy, however, the location of the family (*beth-av*) at the center of the constellation of Israelite social institutions was over.

Following vast political changes which took place in the near east, the most obvious of which involved the threat of invasion and defeat of Israel by the Philistines, a form of centrally controlled government was inevitable. The new institutions at the center of Israelite culture, the institution which had to survive at the cost of all others, was the state in the form of the eastern monarchy.

As a short-cut to enlighten ourselves as to what the monarchy did to the *beth-av* we should read the warning speech attributed to Samuel in 1 Samuel 8:10–18. We can accept the basic accuracy of this account since it is spoken by Samuel whom the Deuteronomic historian presents as a true prophet, one whose words come true.

> These will be the ways of the king who will reign over you: he will take your sons and appoint them to his chariots and to be his horsemen, and to run before his chariots; and he will appoint for himself commanders of thousands and commanders of fifties, and some to plow his ground and to reap his harvest, and to make his implements of war and the equipment of his chariots. He will take your daughters to be per-

fumers and cooks and bakers. He will take the best of
your fields and vineyards and olive orchards and give
them to his servants. He will take your menservants
and maidservants, and the best of your cattle and
your asses, and put them to his work. He will take the
tenth of your flocks, and you shall be his slaves.

After the coming of the monarchy, the rural residents of
Israel found themselves in a position similar to the Hebrews
of Egypt. They had to produce a greater amount with less
resources (Ex 5:7). As time went on, those who worked and
produced had less and less to show for their labor. The power
and wealth of the land became centered in two rich urban
areas, Jerusalem and Samaria. There are some scholars who
believe that Israel emerged as a nation in the highlands during
the thirteenth century as a federation of groups of people who
lived in the highlands in order to avoid living in a feudal relationship with Canaanite city states. If this is true, then we are
examining one of the ironies of history. By the middle of the
eighth century when Amos appeared in the city of Samaria,
the rural residents of the highlands of Israel were back in a
feudal relationship with a city state. This time the residents
of the city state were the rich and powerful of Israel.

CHAPTER IV

The Seventh Century Scribe of Jerusalem

A hundred years after the death of Amos an incident took place in Jerusalem which symbolizes the beginning of a new era for Israel. We are told that when Josiah was king he ordered the cleaning and repair of the Jerusalem temple. During the course of the repairs a scroll was discovered.

> And Hilkiah the high priest said to Shapan the secretary, I have found the book of the law in the house of the LORD (2 Kgs 22:8).

The scroll which was discovered in the temple is commonly identified as the core of the book of Deuteronomy. The reforms which Josiah initiated were all spelled out in Deuteronomy, chapters 12 through 26. There are two "histories" of this period contained in the Bible; one is in the book of Kings and the other in the book of Chronicles. In Kings, the discovery of the scroll triggers the extensive reforms of the cult of Yahweh by King Josiah which made him the perfect hero of the Deuteronomistic historian.

> Before him there was no king like him, who turned to the LORD with all his heart and with all his soul and with all his might, according to all the law of Moses; nor did any like him arise after him (2 Kgs 23:25).

In Chronicles the reforms of Josiah were reported to have been already in progress when the scroll was discovered. In this version, the scroll (called the book of the law) supported the reforms, but did not trigger them.

Regardless of which version is accurate, one thing is evident. The age of the *written* word of God had begun. Up until this time in the Bible history there had been no written document recognized as the word of God. Yahweh had spoken to his people in many ways—for example:

(a) With a voice of his own (Ex 20:1).
(b) Through dreams (Gen 28:12).
(c) Through visions (Gen 15:1).
(d) Through divine messengers (angels).
(e) Through the voice of human mediators (prophets).

But now the written document was becoming a medium of Yahweh's revelation. We know there had been many written materials before the days of Josiah, of course, which *later* became part of our Bible. For example, two of these written documents are now identified as "J" and "E." The J document is so named because of the name used for God (Jahweh, in German). It is believed to have been produced during the reign of Solomon by a Jerusalem author. The E document is so named because the name of God is El or Elohim. E is thought to have been authored by someone in the northern kingdom of Israel (sometimes called Ephraim), possibly in the days of Amos. What we don't know about these documents is how they were circulated before this time (if they were circulated), who had them, who read them, and how they were viewed.

Was there an incident before the days of Josiah when written words on a scroll were recognized as the method by which Yahweh was speaking to his people? In Joshua 24, after Joshua finished summarizing the history of his people and challenged them to choose Yahweh and remain true to him, Joshua ". . . wrote these words in the book of the law of Yahweh." This is an idealization of the past. At any rate there is no account in the Bible of anyone reading this book of Joshua's. We can say with assurance that during the seventh century in Israel, in conjunction with the new nationalism of Josiah and the growth of the centralized, Deuteronomic movement, writing came into its own as a centrally important vehicle of learning about the invisible God and the will of this God in Judah.

The Emergence of the Scribe as Theologian

It was in Jerusalem in the seventh century that a new and important role for the scribe emerged on the stage of Israel's religious history. In conjunction with the same forces which gave birth to the Deuteronomic school, the importance of writings grew, and as it did the role of the scribe evolved into something new. There had been secretaries/scribes from the beginning of the monarchy. Scribes were the experts who mastered the art of writing. They had become responsible for everything connected with writing, the preservation of older documents, the copying of existent scrolls for circulation and future use, the creation of new writings. It is natural that in the days of Josiah, in conjunction with the religious reforms of the crown, the role of the scribe would be enhanced. I am suggesting this: during the reign of Josiah secretaries or scribes who were supported by the monarchy to record everything that was required for the welfare of the state became religious specialists also, and some of them became the official theologians of Judah.

It would be helpful to have detailed information concerning the day-to-day life and activity of the scribes. Who supported them, and how well were they supported? How much freedom did they have? What was their relationship to the priesthood? What was their place in the royal court? What was their social location in Jerusalem?

Unfortunately, we do not have extensive information to answer these questions in detail with assurance. We have to speculate concerning some activities of the scribes based on related information at our disposal. I suspect that because of their ability to read and write so well, scribes became the official readers at state supported religious ceremonies. We do know that some scribes grew into positions of leadership.

After the captivity of Judah, during the restoration period, Ezra the scribe was a recognized teacher and leader of the returnees. Scribes became knowledgeable about the content of the scriptures they copied and edited, so that it could be said of Ezra:

> —this Ezra went up from Babylonia. He was a scribe skilled in the law of Moses. . . . For Ezra had set his heart to study the law of the LORD, and to do it, and to teach his statutes and ordinances in Israel (Ezr 7:6, 10).

Seventh Century Political Situation

It is necessary to know something of the political situation at this time. The predictions of Amos of Tekoa had come true. The city of Samaria was completely destroyed in 722 B.C.E. and the northern kingdom of Israel became a western territory of Assyria. Those who were able to escape fled to Judah. This probably involved no small number.

But early in the seventh century the Assyrian empire showed signs of weakening, and by the middle of the century the sprawling power from the east was in trouble. It is not our concern to enumerate the details of Assyria's decline. It is sufficient for us to know that the little kingdom of Judah was virtually free of Assyrian domination when Josiah became king in 640 B.C.E. Josiah was able to capitalize on Assyria's weakness. In the early reign of Josiah there was a great optimism concerning the re-establishment of Israel as it had been in the days of David. Judah was going to annex the land to its north which had formerly belonged to the kingdom of united Israel.

The Deuteronomic movement may have been more than the religious arm of Josiah's actions. It may have been the motivator of the whole military, political, and economic movement toward the recapture of Israel's old glory. Presenting itself as an obstacle to the Deuteronomic goal of complete centralization of Yahweh worship in Jerusalem was the shrine of Bethel, the most significant of the high places. Located only

ten miles from Jerusalem, north of the border of Judah, Bethel
was a popular place of worship with a tradition in Israel which
pre-dated Jerusalem. It was at Bethel that Jacob dreamed of a
ladder which extended to the heavens. Popular etymology
stated that Jacob gave the site the name of Bethel the morning
following his dream.

The Bethel Passages

To implement the Josianic/Deuteronomic purpose Bethel
had to be both destroyed and discredited. The oracles of Amos
would be extremely helpful in discrediting Bethel. Wolff
writes, "In the days of Josiah ... the book of Amos was
searched so thoroughly for references to Bethel, or even
merely to an 'altar,' that no passage was overlooked which
lent itself to interpretation in light of Josiah's action."[1]

In the Deuteronomic history we read in 1 Kings:

> And behold, a man of God came out of Judah by the
> word of the Lord to Bethel. Jeroboam was standing by
> the altar to burn incense. And the man cried against
> the altar by the word of the LORD, and said "O altar,
> altar, thus says the LORD: 'Behold, a son shall be born
> to the house of David, Josiah by name; and he shall
> sacrifice upon you the priests of the high places who
> burn incense upon you, and men's bones shall be
> burned upon you.' ... Behold, the altar shall be torn
> down, and the ashes that are upon it shall be poured
> out" (1 Kgs 13:1–3).

If Amos of Tekoa had prophesied against the capital city of
Israel, Samaria, it is possible he also prophesied against
Bethel, ". . . the king's sanctuary . . . a temple of the [northern]
kingdom." In the oracles of Amos of Tekoa which Coote has
identified there are no references to Bethel. Wolff says that
only one Bethel passage can be attributed to Amos with assurance (4:4–5). It is quite possible that the Bethel passages were
the first seventh century additions to the oracles of the

prophet of Tekoa. They may have been based on oral traditions concerning Amos. In the description of Josiah's reform-
ing actions Bethel is singled out:

> Moreover the altar at Bethel, the high place erected
> by Jeroboam ... who made Israel to sin, that altar
> with the high place he [Josiah] pulled down and he
> broke in pieces its stones, crushing them to dust ...
> and he sent and took the bones out of the tombs, and
> burned them upon the altar, and defiled it, according
> to the word of the LORD which the man of God pro-
> claimed, who had predicted these things (2 Kgs
> 23:15–16).

The great reformation of Josiah seemed to be moving ahead
with great success when it suddenly came to a crashing halt.
Something happened which changed everything:

> Pharaoh Neco king of Egypt went up to the king of
> Assyria. King Josiah went to meet him; and Pharaoh
> Neco slew him at Megiddo. ... His servants carried
> him dead in a chariot from Megiddo, and brought him
> to Jerusalem, and buried him in his own tomb (2 Kgs
> 23:29).

In one day, the hope and optimism of seventh century Judah
was drained, and Jerusalem shortly thereafter became a vassal
of Egypt. After the death of Josiah the Bible history found in
both the books of Kings and Chronicles comes to a surpris-
ingly quick end. In just a few paragraphs we are told about
Judah's troubles, first with Egypt and then with Neo-
Babylonia.

Reviving the Oracles of Amos of Tekoa

With the possibility of the destruction of Judah on the not-
so-distant horizon, a scribe of Jerusalem, now familiar with
the oracles of Amos of Tekoa (because of the Bethel expan-

sion), saw the value of continuing a seventh century edition
of Amos. Here was a prophet who had predicted the destruction of Samaria. Perhaps his words, now a hundred years old,
should be widely heard again. If they were updated to appeal
to the Judahites of this age, they would still carry the power
of Yahweh's words. So, it is my belief, a scribe of Jerusalem
appropriated the words of a prophet from a previous century,
and carefully and lovingly placed them into a Deuteronomic
structure which would have the effect of convincing the
hearts and souls of Yahweh's people to turn once again to
Yahweh for his salvation.

We will now look at several of the ways in which the scribe
accomplished his goal. We will also find that as a result of his
process his new book of Amos would say things that Amos of
Tekoa did not say, and probably had not even thought about.

Here are five areas on which we will comment:

(a) Hymnic material.
(b) Respect for the office of prophet.
(c) A response expected.
(d) Fondness for the number five.
(e) Wisdom literature.

Hymnic Material

This is a good place to start. Almost all commentators recognize the placing of hymnic matter from the Jerusalem cult
of Yahweh into the book of Amos. The example is as follows:

> The LORD roars from Zion
>   and utters his voice from Jerusalem;
> the pastures of the shepherds mourn,
>   and the top of Carmel withers (1:2).

The other hymnic insertions are found in 4:13, 5:8f, 9:5f, and
possibly 8:8. Although this is speculation, it is not outside the
realm of possibility that the hymnic materials were sung by a
choir (possibly made up of male and female voices) at a public

service where the oracles of Amos were read by a scribe. After all, if the book of Amos was expanded by a seventh century scribe of Jerusalem as we are suggesting, it had to have an audience of some kind. The scribe didn't do all this work for his own edification.

It would work something like this. The reader would read the expanded introduction (note the brackets supplied by Wolff)

> The words of Amos [who was among the sheep breeders,] from Tekoa which he viewed concerning Israel [in the days of Uzziah king of Judah and in the days of Jeroboam the son of Joash, king of Israel,] two years before the earthquake (Am 1:1),

after which the choir would sing or chant

> "The LORD roars from Zion
>   and utters his voice from Jerusalem;
> the pastures of the shepherds mourn,
>   and the top of Carmel withers" (Am 1:2),

and this would continue, reading, choral response, reading, choral response, for the complete reading with the choir singing each hymnic insertion. In the book of Ezra we have a list of temple personnel: priests, Levites, gatekeepers, singers, and temple servants (Ezr 7:73). And of course we have references to choirmasters in the introductions to many psalms.

Note the same theme of Yahweh's control over nature, which runs through the verses of hymn:

> . . . the top of Carmel withers (1:2).

> he who forms the mountains . . .
> and treads on the heights of the earth (4:13).

> and darkens the day into night,
> who calls for the waters of the sea, and pours them out upon the surface of the earth (5:8).

who touches the earth and it melts,
the LORD is his name (9:5–6).

The book of Amos which I am suggesting was read at a public service was not as long as the book of Amos in its final version. Now if you are alert you may ask a question at this point.
This hymn is about Yahweh's power over nature, and that
was not one of the themes of Amos of Tekoa. Why did the
scribe choose this hymn? Wasn't there a hymn more
appropriate?

Perhaps the answer lies in the opening words of the hymn
where Yahweh "roars" (like a lion) from Zion. In chapter 3 the
scribe added these words: "The lion has roared; who will not
fear?" (3:8). In the oracles of Amos there are several references to lions. Amos, speaking of the sureness of Yahweh's
judgment, says, "It is as if a man fled from a lion, and a bear
met him" (5:19). In another scene Amos speaking vividly of
Samaria's destruction says:

> Thus says the Lord: "As a shepherd rescues from the
> mouth of the lion two legs, or a piece of an ear, so
> shall the people of Israel who dwell in Samaria be
> rescued, with the corner of a couch and part of a bed"
> (3:12).

The least that can be said for the inserted hymnic material
is that it is an uneasy mix with the oracles of Amos of Tekoa;
but this argues for a later insertion. These words were not the
words of the original prophet.

Respect for the Office of Prophet

The social location of the prophet in ancient Israel has been
the subject of a fine study by Robert R. Wilson in his book
Prophecy and Society in Ancient Israel.[2] The behavior of the
prophet and how the prophet was viewed by the people of
Israel varied from time to time and from place to place.

The seventh century Deuteronomic school had its own

view of the ideal prophet which appears throughout the Deuteronomistic history, not to mention in the stories of Elijah
and Elisha. Here is an example of the Deuteronomistic reports
concerning prophetic activity:

> Yet the LORD warned Israel and Judah by every
> prophet and every seer, saying, "Turn from your evil
> ways and keep my commandments and my statutes,
> in accordance with all the law which I commanded
> your fathers, and which I sent to you by my servants
> the prophets" (2 Kgs 17:13).

Some scholars have seen in the third person narrative story
of Amos and Amaziah (Am 7:10–17) the Deuteronomic picture
of the rejected prophet.

So it is not unexpected that the scribe we are picturing
would insert some statements concerning the role of prophets
in the new book of Amos. After all, Amos was a true prophet
according to the implied definition in Deuteronomy where the
reader is told how to identify a false prophet:

> And if you say in your heart, "How may we know the
> word which the LORD has not spoken?"—when a
> prophet speaks in the name of the LORD, if the word
> does not come to pass or come true, that is a word
> which the LORD has not spoken; the prophet has spo-
> ken it presumptuously, you need not be afraid of him
> (Dt 18:21–22).

This may be the place to make a comment about a paragraph which has inspired hundreds of scholarly pages. During
the encounter with Amaziah, Amos says "I am not a prophet
(nabi)." He then goes on to tell how he was called by Yahweh
to deliver his prophetic message while he was following the
flock. (Similar words are used about David in 1 Kings 7:8
where Yahweh is quoted as saying to David, "I took you from
the pasture, from following the sheep.")

Studying this passage to determine, in the eyes of the Deuteronomic scribe, whether Amos was trying to disassociate himself from other prophets can lead us into a semantic maze. I think the best solution is this: he acts like a prophet, he preaches like a prophet, so therefore he must be a prophet. Besides a book in the Old Testament has been built on his oracles.

Editorial comments added to the oracles of Amos concerning the prophets include the following:

> Surely the Lord God does nothing, without revealing his secret to the prophets (Am 3:7).

> And I raised up some of your sons for prophets. . . . But you made the Nazarites drink wine and commanded the prophets saying "You shall not prophesy" (Am 2:11–12).

Amos of Tekoa said nothing about the prophets in his original oracles. As can be seen from our view of the seventh century edition of Amos, the sins of the Israelites are expanded to include rejection of the prophet. The end result is to dilute the intensity of the original indictment concerning the intolerable exploitation of the poor and the weak by the urban rich and powerful, the ruling elite.

A Response Expected

The literature of the Deuteronomic school expects a response from the readers and listeners. As you read Deuteronomic scripture you are constantly challenged to do something:

- take heed
- learn them (the laws)
- be careful to do them (the laws)
- make them known
- teach your children
- repent

- turn back to Yahweh
- make a choice.

Some scholars have pointed out that even the Deutero-nomic history (the earliest form of which emerged in the seventh century during and after the reign of Josiah) has the expectation of a response from the people. Wolff in an essay entitled "The Kerygma of the Deuteronomic Work"[3] refers to the Deuteronomic prayer of Solomon at the dedication of the temple in 1 Kings 8 to illustrate the theme of repentance and return to Yahweh which the D history promotes and proposes. Solomon prays:

> When thy people Israel are defeated before the enemy because they have sinned against thee, if they turn again to thee, and acknowledge thy name, and pray and make supplication to thee in this house; then hear thou in heaven, and forgive the sin of thy people Israel, and bring them again to the land which thou gavest to their fathers (1 Kgs 8:33–34; see also vv. 46–53).

The theme of the benefits of repenting and returning to Yahweh is hammered at the reader in the book of Judges.

Now you may be saying to yourself, of course, that most of scripture expects and encourages a response from its readers. What is the point of this discussion? The point is that we are not comparing the second layer of the book of Amos with "most of scripture." We are comparing it with the oracles of Amos of Tekoa. And Amos of Tekoa did not expect a response from his audience. Read carefully these words of Robert Coote:

> Amos's oracles imply no response, have no future, offer no program, and leave no room for repentance. They lead directly to an absolute dead end.[4]

Amos did not prophesy expecting wholesale repentance or

even a small response. Why then did he prophesy? This is an important question which we will discuss in chapter VII. At the present time we will continue to look at the seventh century additions to the book of Amos which expect or hope for a response.

Here are some exhortations added to Amos by the scribe:

Seek me and live; but do not seek Bethel (5:5).

Seek good and not evil, that you may live (5:14).

Hate evil, and love good, and establish justice in the gate (5:15).

. . . let justice roll down like waters, and righteousness like an ever flowing stream (5:24).

There are several things to notice about these seventh century exhortations. The first one (Seek me and live) should remind us of Deuteronomy 4:29 which reads, "You will seek the LORD your God and you will find him."

But of much greater importance, notice the vocabulary of the scribe: good, evil, justice, righteousness. This is not the vocabulary of the prophet from Tekoa. These words are abstractions. They are vague. Every reader who is in favor of *good* please raise your hand. Now, every reader who is opposed to *evil*, raise your hand. (See what I mean?)

These abstract words do serve a purpose. If you are talking about economic injustice, you can't specifically list several examples of unfairness in your society every time you refer to these practices. Every language has general terms which put things into categories. What I am saying is that Amos of Tekoa did not use these abstract words. The oracles of Amos are earthy and specific. He condemned merchants who could not wait for the sabbath to be over so that they could—

. . . make the ephah small and the shekel great,
   and deal deceitfully with false balances,

that we may buy the poor for silver
  and the needy for a pair of sandals,
  and sell the refuse of the wheat (8:5-6).

There is nothing abstract about these charges. Amos does not charge the merchants with being evil or unjust. He describes in detail their behavior. Another example of Amos' specificity and detail:

Woe to those who lie on beds of ivory . . .
who sing idle songs to the sound of the harp
who drink wine in bowls
  and anoint themselves with the finest oils
  but are not grieved over the ruin of Joseph (6:4-6).

It is not difficult to perceive the difference between these two literary styles, and when you do you are in a position to identify a basic difference between the first two layers of the book of Amos. The scribe was writing for a different audience. For one thing the scribe is not as concerned about the exploitation of the rural peasants by the rich and powerful. On the other hand, the scribe is employed and supported by the elite of Jerusalem. Perhaps you have noticed that there is a compassion for the poor and needy in the Deuteronomic writings. It is a truism that the school of Deuteronomy was influenced by the eighth century prophets. But the compassion of Deuteronomy is closer to what we think of today as charity. The poor, the widow, the alien should receive some of the harvest. This sentiment is expressed in several of the Deuteronomic laws—for example:

When you reap your harvest in your field, and have forgotten a sheaf in the field, you shall not go back to get it; it shall be for the sojourner, the fatherless, and the widow. . . . When you gather grapes of your vineyard, you shall not glean it afterward; it shall be for the sojourner, the fatherless, and the widow (Dt 24:19-21).

If we wanted to be cynical we could say that the poor are
entitled to the crumbs which fall from the master's table. The
Deuteronomist may have believed that the society of Judah
was the best of all societies. We must keep in mind that Deuteronomy is primarily interested in the survival of the nation,
the people of Yahweh. When the nation is destroyed, then the
Deuteronomist wants above all for the reader to understand,
first, that Yahweh's mighty hand and arm are not weakened,
but that the nation deserved his wrath, and, second, that if the
people turn to Yahweh with confession and prayer he may
restore them to the land.

The scribe believes that the society of Judah is worth sav-
ing, and the fact that he is expanding the oracles of Amos may
indicate that he has more of a social conscience than we give
him credit for. We will discuss this further in our chapter VII.

Fondness for the Number Five

In the seventh century edition of Amos there are several
groupings of five. In chapter 4 there are references to five judgments which came in the past. Each judgment ends with the
words ". . . yet you did not return to me." (Returning to Yahweh is a Deuteronomic theme.) There are five visions, the first
beginning with the words:

> Thus the Lord God showed me: behold, he was form-
> ing locusts in the beginning of the shooting up of the
> latter growth (Am 7:1).

And although the present book begins with eight oracles
against the nations, almost every scholar separates three
(Edom, Tyre, and Judah) from the rest. And that leaves five. I
believe that the scribe is responsible for the five original oracles against the nations. They are Damascus, Gaza, the
Ammonites, Moab, and Israel. You should ask at this point
"Why did the scribe start his edition of Amos with five oracles
against the nations?" Does the geographical location of these
nations give us a clue? Damascus was north, Gaza to the west,
Ammon and Moab to the east, and Israel in the center.

I am not sure that we have a convincing answer for this question. We have already mentioned that the oracle against a foreign nation was a form characteristic of the Jerusalem cult of Yahweh.[5] Perhaps placing the oracles first was a sure-fire way to get the attention of the audience at that time. Today the oracles against the nations number eight (five plus three added later) and they seem to have a discouraging effect on the modern reader who is hardly interested in these ancient countries. We can say with some assurance that this was not the effect these pronouncements would have had on seventh century B.C.E. hearers or readers.

There is some art involved in the way the scribe deals with the fifth nation, Israel. After its ritual words of introduction (for three transgressions of Israel, and for four, I will not revoke the punishment), the fifth oracle begins with the words of Amos of Tekoa. This is the first appearance of Amos' words in this seventh century edition.

Perhaps there was some ancient logic that suggested that circling Israel, then stopping there was the way to make a point. All Judeans would be familiar with the fate of the northern kingdom. One important effect has to be noted. The scribe puts Israel in the class with four pagan nations. And this type of comparison is repeated in the book of Amos later, in another scribal addition.

> "Are you not like the Ethiopians to me,
>   O people of Israel?" says the LORD.
> "Did I not bring up Israel from the land of Egypt,
>   and the Philistines from Caphtor and the Syrians from
>   Kir" (Am 9:7)?

Why did the scribe like five? It may have something to do with his being a writer. Whereas some preachers have been known to favor three point sermons, perhaps there is something about the number five which feels right to some writers—at least for short works. It has been pointed out that one of the authors of the Penteteuch, the priestly writer (called P), had a fondness for the number ten. There are ten genealogies spread out throughout his work. And in his account of creation we read ten times "And Elohim said." Could it be related to the fact that we have five fingers on one hand, and ten on two?

Wisdom Literature

Wisdom literature is found dispersed throughout the book of Amos. Wisdom literature usually consists of wise sayings, sometimes in a string. These sayings are rhythmic and frequently make comparisons. For example:

> A word fitly spoken
> is like apples of gold in a setting of silver (Prov 25:11).

Sometimes there is no comparison:

> Pride goes before destruction,
> and a haughty spirit before a fall.

Sometimes they are moral:

> Diverse weights are an abomination to the LORD
> and false scales are not good.

H.W. Wolff wrote a book called *Amos the Prophet, The Man and His Background.*[6] This book is entirely devoted to an explanation of the relationship between wisdom literature and the prophet Amos.

Our belief is that almost all of the examples of wisdom literature found in the book of Amos were added by the seventh century scribe. Here are some examples:

> Do two walk together,
> unless they have made an appointment (3:3)?

> Does a bird fall in a snare on the earth
> when there is no trap for it (3:5)?

They hate him who reproves in the gate
and they abhor him who speaks the truth (5:10).

Do horses run upon rocks?
Does one plow the sea with oxen?
But you have turned justice into poison
and the fruit of righteousness into wormwood (6:12).

There is another element of wisdom literature found in the book of Amos. It is called the numerical sequence. There are several types found in the proverbs. For example:

Three things are too wonderful for me;
four I do not understand
the way of an eagle in the sky,
the way of a serpent on a rock
the way of a ship on the high seas,
and the way of a man with a maid (Prov 30:18–19).

There are six things which the LORD hates
seven which are an abomination to him (Prov 6:16).

The oracles against the nations in chapters 2 and 3 of Amos all begin with a numerical sequence statement.

For three transgressions of [name of nation],
and for four I will not revoke the punishment.

There are some problems with the scribe's decision to use wisdom literature in his structure for the oracles of Amos. Wisdom literature has a feeling and a philosophy which is entirely foreign to the fiery oracles of Amos of Tekoa. Wisdom is clever for its own sake. When wisdom sayings are used they are supposed to end the argument and calm the disturbance. The wise man tells the poor to remember: "He who trusts in his riches will wither, but the righteous will flourish like a green leaf" (Prov 11:28). To the hungry he says to remember:

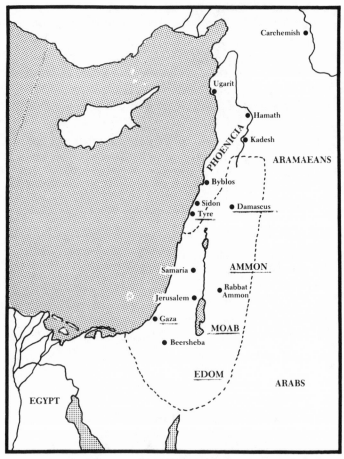

Notice how the six foreign nations mentioned in the oracles against the nations in Amos, Chapters 1 and 2, surround Samaria (Israel) and Jerusalem (Judah). Also notice that in those days a nation was sometimes referred to by the name of its chief city, for example Damascus for Syria.

"Better is a dinner of herbs where love is, than a fatted ox and hatred with it" (Prov 15:17). Does this sound like Amos to you?

Now to be sure the above two examples are extreme to make a point. The scribe did not select these words for his structure, so I suggest that you look at the words he did select as noted previously.

Here is a question. Why would a seventh century scribe decide to put the oracles of Amos, specific and biting as they are, in a literary structure containing wisdom style literature known for its timelessness and generality? The answer may lie in the question. He would do it for the same reason he used vague, abstract terms like justice and righteousness. He wanted his edition of Amos to appeal to a wider, universal audience. The end of the kingdom of Judah may have appeared inevitable, or may already have taken place. He wanted his scroll to survive in value for future generations. Our scribe should be given credit for his success. Today, millennia later, few among us have not quoted or listened with excitement to his words:

But let justice roll down like waters
and righteousness like an ever-flowing stream (5:24).

CHAPTER V

The Final Author
of the Book of Amos

Sixty years after the completion of the second edition of the book of Amos the majesty of Jerusalem was only a memory and many of the former inhabitants of Judah had died in Babylonian captivity. The destruction of Jerusalem and the deportation of her chief families had taken place in several stages between the years 598 and 582 B.C.E. But the destruction had been thorough.

> Nebuzaradan ... a servant of the king of Babylon, came to Jerusalem. And he burned the house of the LORD, and the king's house and all the houses of Jerusalem; every great house he burned down. And all the army of the Chaldeans ... broke down the walls around Jerusalem (2 Kgs 25:9–10).

If the seventh century scribe of Jerusalem hoped that the response of the Judahites to his edition of Amos would enable the kingdom of Judah to escape the fate of the northern kingdom, Israel, he was wrong. There was an important difference however for these Jewish exiles. The captivity in Babylon turned out to be a somewhat humane experience for the Jews compared with the fate of the northern Israelites of a previous century. After the early years of inevitable chaos in Babylon, about which we have little information, the Jews were allowed to lead normal family lives. Religious leaders were allowed to speak freely, and the exiles communicated with Jews who remained in Judah. A window through which we

56

can view aspects of life in Babylon can be found in words of advice to the exiles from Jeremiah:

> Build houses and live in them; plant gardens and eat their produce. Take wives and have sons and daughters . . . multiply there, and do not decrease. But seek the welfare of the city where I have sent you into exile, and pray to the LORD on its behalf, for in its welfare you will find your welfare (29:5).

One momentous result of the captivity period was a phenomenon which was going to influence the history of civilization for thousands of years. The captives, deprived of their king and their freedom, the city of Jerusalem and the temple, learned to treasure the one thing they were able to take with them to Babylon, their religious writings. These writings, some of which would become "holy" scriptures for millions of people in the future, were read, searched, studied, memorized and adored. Some of the scrolls would be expanded and updated. Several of these scrolls were based on the oracles of the eighth century prophets. The second edition of the book of Amos was one of them.

Three More Oracles Against the Nations

The scribe of Jerusalem had formed five oracles against the nations to begin his book of Amos. The fifth nation was Israel. After introducing the fifth oracle with the words:

> For three transgressions of Israel
>   and for four, I will not revoke the punishment (2:6),

the scribe used the words of Amos of Tekoa to describe the sins of Israel's capital city Samaria. Now, in the sixth century, three more oracles were added; the sixth century redactor had no interest in preserving the number five. The three later oracles were against Tyre, Edom, and Judah. Notice that each of these three *end* with a prediction that "the strongholds" of the nation will be destroyed. In the earlier oracles the mention of strongholds is at the mid-point of the oracle.

The oracle against Edom is understandable. In the final stages of Judah's destruction by the Chaldeans in 586 B.C.E. Edom moved into southern Judah and claimed parts for its own. Edom may even have assisted in the defeat of Judah. Obadiah writes:

> For the violence done to your brother Jacob . . .
> You should not have looted his goods in the day of his
>   calamity.
> You should not have stood at the parting of the ways to
>   cut off his fugitives
> You should not have delivered up his survivors in the
>   day of distress (10:13–14).

The reason for the oracle against Tyre is obscure. Tyre was an important seacoast city in Phoenicia. Because Tyre "delivered up a whole people to Edom" this somehow indicated a failure to remember "the covenant of brotherhood." Wolff says: "The expression 'to remember a covenant' is unattested in preexilic material but is relatively frequent in the Priestly work."[1] If Tyre is used for the name of Phoenicia (a common practice was to use the chief city name for the whole country), then a look at the map at the end of the last chapter will show that the six countries named in the oracles completely surround Israel and Judah. Perhaps Tyre was added to complete a circle.

Since the readers of the final book of Amos would be former citizens of Judah, it was inevitable that an oracle be directed against Judah. Like the other two new oracles, this one significantly ends with the strongholds being destroyed. The sin of Judah is described in Deuteronomic language.

> —because they have rejected the law of the LORD.
>   and have not kept his statutes,
> but their lies have led them astray,
>   after which their fathers walked.

This oracle differs from the original five of the previous century; each of them listed at least one *specific* crime against persons. The accusation of not keeping Yahweh's statutes could mean almost anything. On the other hand, the audience for this version of Amos would already have been familiar with the many and various sins of Judah.

Coote suggests that the name "Zion" may have been inserted in the famous "woe" statement at this stage.

Woe to those who are at ease in Zion (6:1).

Yahweh's Final Words in Amos

Strange as it may seem, theological developments which took place during the period of the Babylonian exile had their foundation in the oracles of Amos of Tekoa. Amos had made it very clear that it was Yahweh who would destroy Israel for her sins. When the prediction of Amos came true, that is, when the Assyrians completely destroyed Samaria and carried away the powerful elite, the Assyrians were only carrying out the will of Yahweh. Israel was destroyed, not because Yahweh was absent or impotent, but expressly because Yahweh was present and powerful. That is why in Amos the day of Yahweh was darkness for the Israelites and not light.

If you could understand the role of Yahweh in Israel's destruction, then you could understand it for Judah also. Was Judah destroyed because Yahweh had lost interest or lacked the power to save Judah? (Had Yahweh's hand waxed short?) The answer is no. The destruction of Judah was a manifestation of Yahweh's will and a fulfillment of his word.

The other side of this theological coin was this: If Yahweh was powerful to destroy, then Yahweh was powerful to rebuild.

As time went on in the exilic community faith triumphed over despair. The growth of an optimistic faith, the kind of faith that sometimes grows paradoxically in times of great adversity, bolstered by various problems for the conquering Babylonians, problems concerning internal economic, military, and political developments, resulted in a religion for Yahweh's people permeated with hope. Old men began to dream dreams, and young men began to see visions. A new and powerful interest in the old tradition of Israel concerning the exodus became the center for new and glorious oracles of a new prophet whose name we do not know, but whose poetry became an extension of the book of Isaiah. As if the Judahites were ashamed and guilty for having doubted the power of Yahweh during the early days of captivity, they developed a new appreciation of his power, a power which now reached in so many directions that it could only be described as universal, and reached back in time to the days of creation.

The sixth century edition of Amos (containing the eighth century oracles of Amos in the elaborate seventh century framework discussed in chapter IV) was expanded to include a closing oracle of salvation which reflected the renewed faith and hope of the captivity community.

> "In that day I will raise up
>   the booth of David that is fallen
> and repair its breaches,
>   and raise up its ruins,
>   and rebuild it as in days of old. . . ."

> "Behold the days are coming," says the LORD,
>   "when the plowman shall overtake the reaper
>   and the treader of grapes him who sows the seed;
> the mountains shall drip sweet wine,
>   and all the hills shall flow with it.
> I will restore the fortunes of my people Israel
>   and they shall rebuild the ruined cities and inhabit
>   them. . . ."
> "They shall plant vineyards and drink their wine,
>   and they shall make gardens and eat their fruit.
> I will plant them upon their land,
>   and they shall never again be plucked up
>   out of the land which I have given them,"
>   says the LORD your God.

The first thing to notice about this passage is that it presupposes the destruction of Judah and a need for a restoration. Casual readers of the book of Amos may be inclined to disregard this closing oracle, regarding it as something foreign to the body of the book, an artificial closing tacked on to the end of the scroll to add an element of grace to a book top-heavy with wrath and justice. I will try to show that this ending is entirely appropriate.

First there are several reversals to note. Amos of Tekoa had said to his audience, "You have planted pleasant vineyards, but you shall *not* drink their wine." The final author would reverse this for the returnees to Jerusalem:

> They shall plant vineyards and (shall) drink their wine,
>   and they shall make gardens and eat their fruit (9:14).

Keep in mind that the first audience (eighth century) had consisted of the elite, powerful urban oppressors of the rural residents of Israel, the citizens of Samaria. This final audience is again the elite (the elite of Judah or their descendants) but now this society consists of the weak and oppressed. The first had become the last.

Notice how completely agricultural the closing oracle of salvation is. This is especially appropriate if we understand how deeply rooted the original oracles of Amos of Tekoa were in ancient, pre-monarchical Israel, an Israel whose society was completely agricultural, and whose institutions were perfectly balanced to support a large population in a difficult environment, the highlands of Canaan.

The monarchy had emerged in Israel to meet challenges to the federation of heterogeneous groups which for two hundred years had been known as Israel.[2] These challenges were related to political, economic, and military realities of a new age. Eventually, both monarchies substituted centralized, urban control for the *decentralized sharing of power* which had been a chief characteristic of the federation of old Israel. New social objectives, based on a new institution, the *state*, were superimposed on the nation's agricultural base. In pre-monarchical Israel, all institutions had developed to support and strengthen the central institution of the inter-generational family, the *beth-av*. The needs of the *beth-av* had been paramount. By the end of Solomon's reign, 931 B.C.E., the paramount, central institution, the one with needs which had to be met at any cost, was the state in the form of the eastern monarchy. The agricultural institutions found themselves reconstellated by an urban-based power structure which considered itself as in command of the destiny of the culture. Surrounding the throne, and demanding the material support and labor of the citizenry, could be found the royal family, with its luxurious desires, a professional military establishment, a merchant class, and a new elite class of landowners.

Traits of society which the centralized state reinforced and which ran counter to the values of the old egalitarian federation included class stratification, military imperialism, a command economy for the benefit of international trade conducted by and for a small powerful elite class, and the establishment of a feudal relationship between the state and the farmers of Israel. It had been for the purpose of ending or avoiding a similar feudal relationship with the Canaanite city-states that the old federation, first called Israel, had come into existence.

Economic injustice can be defined as an unfair and unequal distribution of nature's resources. The end result of economic injustice in ancient Israel was similar to economic injustice in all third world countries today. A small portion of the population prospered and lived in luxury at the expense of a much larger rural population. It was in the environment of human suffering, suffering caused by the exploitation of human resources, the output of the earth, and the taking away of the land itself from families which had owned it for centuries that the word of Yahweh came to Amos of Tekoa as he was following the flock.

By the end of the sixth century however, as the Babylonian captivity drew to a close, the people of Yahweh were now punished and no longer in need of condemnation or rebuke. They needed a word of healing encouragement. Amos would have understood the rural picture of plowing, sowing seed, and the reaping of a bountiful harvest. In this vision the growing season would last so long that when the plowing started, the reaper would hardly have finished gathering the previous year's crops. And notice that it is the booth of David that would be rebuilt, not the throne of David or the kingdom of David. It is a humble word that refers to a temporary structure constructed in the midst of a field to provide shelter for farm workers. This reminds us of David's rural origins. Perhaps the symbol of the hut was selected because it represents a part of Israel's ancient past.

> You shall dwell in booths for seven days; all that are native in Israel shall dwell in booths, that your generations may know that I made the people of Israel dwell in booths when I brought them out of the land of Egypt: I am the LORD your God (Lev 23:42).

And don't miss what may be a significant name for the restored people:

> . . . my people Israel (Am 9:14).

For more than a hundred years after the destruction of Israel (the northern kingdom), Judah survived. During this time, exiles from Israel, and their spiritual descendants from the north, championed their version of the ancient faith of their fathers, a version of the faith which was not entirely compatible with the faith of Judah which was heavily influenced by Jerusalem and the Davidic covenant. In the days of Josiah new theological hope emerged made up of important elements of the north and south and known to us as the Deuteronomic movement. This movement was unable to save Judah from destruction however.

Now, at the end of the exilic period in an oracle dealing with Judah's hope for restoration, the name Israel is used, an ancient more inclusive name which fits well with the late exilic interest in the traditions of this people's ancient past.

Thus far in this book we have divided the book of Amos into three centuries, representing three completely different political and economic environments to present a summary of a three-layers-of-authorship theory of the book of Amos. We now turn to the spiritual significance of this understanding.

CHAPTER VI

When a Book of the Bible
Has Three Authors

It is the glory of God to conceal things,
   but the glory of kings is to search things out (Prov
   25:2)

We live in a glorious time (to borrow a phrase from the above Bible verse). The value which our culture places on scientific and analytical thinking makes it second nature for us to ". . . search things out" and discover the nature of things which have been in our possession for centuries. Our atomistic approach in the study of ancient items in our possession is assisting us to uncover valuable information not only about the items themselves, but about the method of their production and the lives of the people who produced them.

The sociological approach to the study of the Old Testament which has grown considerably during the last decade is closely related to the disciplines of higher criticism which preceded it. The uncovering of the mores, customs and lifestyle of the people of ancient Israel assists us in understanding the books which that culture produced, and understanding how books were produced assists us in understanding the culture. We have become more aware that there were *basic* ways in which the lives of the Israelites differed from ours. One of the differences was the way books were produced.

In Bible Times Books Were Not Written
the Way Books Are Written Today

In our times it is a normal procedure for books to be written by individuals with a strong sense of identity for any number of reasons, including recognition, profit, or public service. A book may go through many drafts before a final version, ready for distribution, is accepted. This version is printed, copyrighted, and distributed by the thousands. The title of the book appears on the cover along with the name of the author. In Bible times nothing resembling the above would take place.

For one thing, in Bible times individualism, such as we know it, did not exist. It would not exist for thousands of years. In Israel a person's sense of identity was not as an individual but as a member of groups. These groups included family, tribe, and nation. When a person participated in the production of a written product (a scroll) there was no such thing as pride of authorship, and in most cases it would not have occurred to the author(s) to put his (or their) name(s) on the work being produced. (For example, the name of the person who wrote Isaiah, chapters 40 to 55 is unknown to us. His magnificent oracles were simply added to an older book associated with Isaiah, an eighth century prophet of Jerusalem, who lived in the days of Amos.)

The production of a book in its final form would involve more than one person and would be an intergenerational process. A book's development from its first edition to its final form could take hundreds of years. When scrolls first began to play a role in the religious life of Israel, some of the dynamics of oral tradition applied. There were regional variations in oral traditions based on the character and needs of the various communities. In other words there was no one authorized version of an oral tradition. It would change from place to place, from age to age. These variations in oral traditions were not capricious or whimsical, however. They developed in accordance with principles related to community needs and community welfare. Depending on circumstances, oral traditions were adjusted, updated, expanded, and otherwise restructured. In other words, one of their attributes was that they were somewhat *dynamic*. They would grow. The same dynamic process took place in the early days of writing.

When scrolls became a part of the logistics of religious life they had attributes similar to the oral tradition. As the circumstances of life changed for the people, scrolls were expanded, updated, and restructured. At first there was not a "final" edition, or even a perceived need for a "final" edition.

Because there was no widespread distribution of scrolls in accordance with market principles, the title of a scroll played a different role in those days. (Today a title is used to promote a book and sell copies. The title of a book on the cover sometimes sells the book.) The purpose of a title for a scroll in Israel was to identify it. When a new scroll was produced it was given a significant name. Sometimes the name consisted only of the first words on the scroll. This name was not changed when the scroll was later expanded. The book of Isaiah is a good example. The first scroll of Isaiah, who lived the same time as Amos, may have been very short. In the days of King Josiah or later, Isaiah was expanded and restructured until it contained chapters 1 through 39. Late in the exile the magnificent chapters 40 through 55 were added. After the return of the Jews to Jerusalem the final chapters were added. The scroll still carried the name of Isaiah.

How Does the Belief in Several Authors Affect Our Belief in Inspired Scriptures?

When we comprehend the truth concerning the origin of Old Testament books it is bound to have some effect on our beliefs. This will depend to an extent on what our previous views were concerning these matters. We may have to do some mental and spiritual stretching exercises, and we may have to regain our balance as we learn to walk on new terrain. There is a great feeling of satisfaction, however, when new assumptions assist us in answering nagging questions concerning the Bible which have been with us for years. Some of these questions we were not even aware of. They were below the surface, giving us a feeling of confusion.

The three-layer theory of authorship does a fine job of making the various portions of the book of Amos fit together and make sense. It also assists us in approaching other Old Testament books with more understanding.

One of the inevitable consequences of distinguishing additional layers of authorship in a Bible book is the propensity to ascribe a superior validity to the words of the first author. For various reasons we want to identify the words of the originating author (in our case Amos of Tekoa) and undervalue the additions of editors and subsequent authors. This is a situation which we must be aware of, not only to fully appreciate the theology of later contributors, but also because only a disciplined effort on our part will enable us to reconstruct the person of the first part about whom we have accumulated illusionary and misleading knowledge. The steps in this exercise may require unlearning things about a "favorite" Bible hero, illusions which we have carried with us from childhood. This *unlearning* experience has its painful moments, but the ultimate result is an exhilarating feeling related to the attainment of clarity and authority.

After the words of the first author are identified, then we are able to move on to a real appreciation of subsequent contributors. In the book of Amos, the seventh century scribe of Jerusalem had important and powerful things to say in the name of Yahweh, as did the final sixth century author. The word of Yahweh was not complete until all three had made their offering.

The Question of Inspiration

Now the question is: How does this new information affect our belief in inspiration of the scriptures? Whatever our view of inspiration, we agree that the Bible is, or contains, God's word, and is or does so in a way that no other book does. We believe with Paul that "all scripture is given by inspiration of God." Inspiration does not mean, however, even for the most conservative view, that God's Spirit used the prophetic authors as robots or automatons. The character of the prophet was not "violated" as he mouthed incoherent words, but on the contrary the inspired words were the author's words based on his real experience and environment. The fact that we have discovered that a Bible book named Amos was produced by a process taking almost two hundred years should not in any way diminish the value of the book or make it any less "God's word." God is the only author who endures from century to century. God is the single author of the book of Amos.

CHAPTER VII

Spiritual Truth
from the Authors of Amos

The purposes of God are accomplished in a period of time which exceeds the lifetime of one person. The book of Amos is an illustration of how a particular book of the Bible was in formation for several centuries. This fact itself carries for us a spiritual truth. Just because a job cannot be completed in one lifetime does not mean that there is not a role for us in addressing painful social or economic problems causing human suffering. During the period of the exile, between the activity of the second author of Amos (the scribe of Jerusalem) and the final author, who added hope to the finished book of Amos, the Jewish understanding of Yahweh grew dramatically. It grew in terms of geography as Yahweh was recognized more and more as having universal power; this understanding also involved new concepts concerning Yahweh's relationship to time. In answer to the impatient question of the faithful,

"How long, O Lord, how long?"

the words of the prophet answered "My ways are not your ways, saith the Lord," and "A thousand years with the LORD are as a day, and a day as a thousand years." Understanding that the development of the book of Amos (along with most other Old Testament books) spanned a period of time exceeding the lifetime of one generation should be the first spiritual lesson we learn. Things take time. God has his own timetable not limited to the short span of human life.

The theological viewpoint of every Old Testament author is

necessarily entwined with the social setting in which the author lived. Since we have said that there are at least three distinct social settings in the history of ancient Israel which contributed to the book of Amos, we must look at the three spiritual perspectives of the authors of Amos separately.

Amos of Tekoa

When you read the oracles of the original eighth century prophet you know you are hearing the words of an angry person. These words are not the words of a casual observer. They are words filled with intense feeling. This preacher has suffered, along with his family, his friends, his people. He speaks with passion:

> Assemble yourselves upon the mountains of Samaria
>   and see the great tumults within her,
>   and the oppression in her midst.

> Thus saith the LORD: "As a shepherd rescues from the mouth of the lion two legs, or a piece of an ear, so shall the people of Israel who dwell in Samaria be rescued, with the corner of a couch and part of a bed. . . .

> "In all the squares there shall be wailing
>   and in all the streets they shall say, 'Alas! Alas!'"

> "I will bring sackcloth upon all loins
>   and baldness on every head;
> I will make it like the mourning for an only son,
>   and the end of it like a bitter day."

The language of Amos of Tekoa is not the language of logic; it is the language of grief. (If we are public representatives of Christ, then it is our responsibility to understand this intensity. As disciples of Christ, it is not our role to be prophets of doom. But until we pass through the period of grief and anger so sensitively portrayed for us in the oracles of Amos of Tekoa, we will not be able to arrive at the strong position of proclaimers of hope.)[1]

The book of Amos comprises less than one half of one percent of the Old Testament. But Amos comes through the chapters of his short book as an assertive rustic poet whose single-purpose message demands our serious attention. His message is that Yahweh is a God of justice who rejects even the people who claim him as their God when these people destroy the fabric of their society by oppressing their fellows. A grossly unjust society could not honor Yahweh or expect his blessing. Amos' message, that our behavior toward our brothers and sisters is a prime and essential element of true religion, is still a powerful but elusive concept.

It is worth remembering that Amos was an outsider to the prosperous marketplace of Samaria, a rural Judean peasant. The editor of the seventh century edition of Amos has him being rebuked and sent home, forbidden to deliver his oracles in Israel, quite possibly based on a valid Amos tradition. The voice of Amos carried the word of Yahweh, but to the rich and powerful Israelites it was an irritant. He was a skeleton at the feast. Many times in history those who have felt the burden of speaking for God have had to deliver unwelcome and disturbing news to the pillars of their society.

Today, millennia later, the world having become a much smaller place, it is possible to think of the nations of the earth as heterogeneous groups, surviving by using the resources of the earth. If we are willing to accept this symbolism, then there is indeed an important message for us from the oracles of Amos. Our nation and other first world nations in the recent past have exploited the resources of the world for their own prosperity. Many critical voices have been raised concerning the conduct of politics and business by the economically strong nations and the effect on the undeveloped nations of the world. The intensity and degree of pain in some anti-American rhetoric may be identical to the pain of Amos. While a large portion of us remain at ease and secure, much of the world is living in disgraceful poverty. Are we able to ask ourselves as citizens of the world, "Are the resources of the global village being distributed equitably?" Is our way of life the equivalent of ". . . drinking wine from ample bowls and anointing ourselves with the finest of oils," while millions are close to starvation, with no possessions but the threadbare clothes which they wear?

It may be that some of the voices critical of our culture are carrying the truth of Yahweh to us. We have been unfair. We have used legal means and illegal means to oppress peoples and pervert justice. We have bribed dictators with large cash gifts and supplied weapons to eliminate peasant uprisings. We have sent the sons of our American families to die in a war to make the world safe for our own brand of business.

At the same time we have discriminated against groups of our own citizens, structuring into our own culture discriminatory and oppressive practices which cause many of our own citizens to lead marginal existences. There is a deadening despair concentrated unfairly in many identifiable groups of people, both in our nation and throughout the world today. Their position in society assuring for them lives of frustration, pain and anger, is not different from the plight of many Israelites in the days of Amos. It is a fact, however, that many Christians, both clergy and laity, are completely unfamiliar with the fact that clear standards and norms of social justice are found at the deepest foundations of our biblical heritage.

Seventh Century Scribe

Here was a scholar who was concerned with preserving and expanding the oracles of the eighth century prophet Amos because he saw their value for the age in which he lived. Amos had spoken to the citizens of Samaria. The scribe knew that he had something to say to the citizens of Judah one hundred years later.

What the scribe did with the written copy of Amos' oracles is not unlike what Bible students and preachers have done thousands of times since then. He wanted to take words and concepts which applied to a previous situation (social unfairness and economic imbalance in eighth century Israel) and apply them to his age. Biblical scholars like to use the word *appropriate* here. You will often read sentences like this in works of scholarship: "The author appropriated a tradition from a previous age in Israel and applied it to his own age." This is what exilic prophets did when they rediscovered the value of the exodus tradition and gave it new meaning for Judah.

This updating, or borrowing from the past to make a needed statement today is similar to what preachers and teachers do all the time, with one important difference. The scribe of Jerusalem was writing a book which would become part of the Bible.

What was the spiritual message which the scribe's words carry to us? For one thing the scribe believed that there was a role for the hearer of oracles of doom. He presented his readers with an open door of opportunity. Whereas Amos of Tekoa expected no response from his hearers, the scribe believed that his readers had the opportunity to benefit from the lesson of Samaria. And so he urged his readers to make decisions:

Seek good and not evil.

Hate evil, and love good,
    and establish justice in the gate.

Seek the Lord and live.

Prepare to meet your God.

Let justice roll down like waters
    and righteousness like an ever-flowing stream.

We have already pointed out that whereas Amos spoke specific words to specific people (the citizens of Samaria), the scribe addressed people generally with abstract words. The words of the scribe are much more general. As a result his words apply to anyone who reads them. Even today his words carry power and conviction to us in their challenge. If he had been specific to particular issues of his day in Judah, his words would not be so clearly understandable as they are. He manages to put us on the spot.

The scribe was part of the Deuteronomic school, and one of the characteristics of the Deuteronomists was to present a choice. Their message was a challenge to the hearers: "Choose you this day whom you will serve." A repeated theme in D writings (Deuteronomic) is to turn back to God, return to Yahweh. This is an open door of opportunity. In the D prayer of Solomon at the dedication of the temple (a very important building for D) we read:

> When thy people Israel are defeated before the enemy because they have sinned against thee, *if they turn again to thee* (italics mine), and acknowledge thy name, and pray and make supplication to thee in this house; then hear thou in heaven, and forgive the sin of thy people Israel, and bring them again to the land which thou gavest to their fathers (1 Kgs 8:33–34).

Perhaps some of us who are familiar with the scriptures do not see *choice* as something which has to be pointed out or highlighted. We take it for granted. The scribe is reminding us that choice is not something that everyone takes for granted. There are many among us who have a need to hear that there is a choice. Many people need to be told that there is an open door before them. They have to be reminded. They have to be told again and again: Don't just stand there; do something.

It is in conjunction with the scribe's theme of returning, or turning to Yahweh that the five judgments of chapter IV are included. Writing in retrospect concerning the northern kingdom of Israel, the scribe cited adverse natural phenomena which Israel should have responded to but did not—for example:

I smote you with blight and mildew;
    I laid waste your gardens and your vineyards;

> your fig trees and your olive trees the locust
>   devoured;
> Yet you did not return to me (Am 4:9).

The scribe is saying to his reader, "Don't be foolish like the citizens of Israel. Recognize warnings. Return to Yahweh."

The Need to Discredit the Altar at Bethel

In the interest of complete national unity of all Israelites, the central goal of the seventh century Deuteronomists found the existence of the altar at Bethel a tremendous, irritating problem. Bethel, although north of the traditional border of Judah in Israel, was only a short distance from Jerusalem. From the Deuteronomic viewpoint, Bethel was not the place chosen by Yahweh where his name would dwell. Bethel was a high place. *Bethel had to be destroyed*. There was a problem, however. Bethel was a very important ancient shrine. It was here that Jacob dreamed of a ladder which reached to heaven with the angels of God ascending and descending on it. When Jacob awoke he said:

> "Surely the Lord is in this place; and I did not know it." And he was afraid and said, "How awesome is this place! This is none other than the house of God, and this is the gate of heaven."
> So Jacob rose early in the morning, and he took the stone which he had put under his head and set it up for a pillar and poured oil on top of it. He called the name of that place Bethel (Gen 28:16–19).

It is not outside the realm of possibility that the whole purpose of renewing the eighth century oracles of Amos of Tekoa by the seventh century scribe of Jerusalem was for the purpose of redirecting Amos' message of Yahweh's wrath from Samaria exclusively to include also the shrine at Bethel. It may be because of this decision by the scribe that we have the oracles of Amos preserved for us. In the light of this information we must reread the scribe's magnificent words concerning unacceptable worship:

> I hate, I despise your feasts,
>> and I take no delight in your solemn assemblies.
>
> Even though you offer me your burnt offerings and
>> cereal offerings, I will not accept them,
>> and the peace offerings of your fatted beasts I will not
>> look upon.
>
> Take away from me the noise of your songs;
>> to the melody of your harps I will not listen.
>
> But let justice roll down like waters,
>> and righteousness as an ever-flowing stream (5:21–24).

Passages with similar ideas to this one are found in all the prophets. For an example we have Isaiah 1:13–17. Notice the use of the abstract words evil, good, and justice which we said earlier were the words of the Deuteronomic scribe:

> Bring no more vain offerings;
>> incense is an abomination to me.
>
> New moon and sabbath and the calling of assemblies—
>> I cannot endure iniquity and solemn assembly.
>
> Your new moons and your appointed feasts my soul
>> hates;
>> they have become a burden to me,
>> I am weary of bearing them.
>
> When you spread forth your hands,
>> I will hide my eyes from you;
>
> Even though you make many prayers, I will not listen;
>> your hands are full of blood. . . .
>
> Cease to do evil, learn to do good;
>> seek justice, correct oppression;
>> defend the fatherless, plead for the widow.

I'm sure you will agree that there is something special about the scribe's passage in Amos which puts it in the category of powerful, profound religious poetry.

Was the seventh century author directing his words only to the ritual activity of Bethel? In other words, if these same activities were carried out at Jerusalem instead of Bethel, would they inherently be pleasingly acceptable to Yahweh and be in accordance with the demands of justice and right-eousness? The appearance of a similar passage in Isaiah (where Bethel was not an issue) would indicate that the passage in Amos was not written to be applied to Bethel exclusively. One characteristic which should be noticed in this passage, which identifies it as Deuteronomic, is that action is expected of the hearer. In a similar Amos passage Yahweh is the actor. Yahweh says:

> I will turn your feasts into mourning,
>   and your songs into lamentation (Am 8:10).

In Amos 5:23 the hearer is expected to be the actor: "Take away from me the noise of your songs."

I believe it is helpful to note a Deuteronomic writing characteristic at this point. In writing about the past, the Deuteronomist was usually directing his message to the present. With this in mind it is possible to see that the Bethel which the scribe is writing about is a combination of Bethel in the times of Amos (eighth century) and Bethel in the author's own time (seventh century). It is in the story of Amos' visit to the shrine at Bethel that Amos is treated rudely by Amaziah the high priest and forbidden to speak the word of Yahweh. And in this story Bethel is identified as "the king's sanctuary." Who was this king? Remember that Bethel was selected by Jeroboam I as one of his official shrines, and for this he is sin-gled out in the D history as ". . . the one who caused Israel to sin."

Perhaps according to his own logic the scribe convincingly linked the ritual activity of Bethel with the elite of Israel, the segment of society condemned by Amos. According to his Deuteronomic logic this was enough to illustrate that religious ritual at this site had to be hypocritical. Participation in the religious festivals and pilgrimages of Israel were supposed to produce a sense of brotherhood and unity with one's fellow worshiper,[2] not support a corrupt society where the urban rich exploited the poor shamelessly and in disregard for the laws of Yahweh which granted the land to all the families of Israel. The fact that Bethel in the past was an official shrine of the destroyed northern kingdom was enough to discredit its rituals.

The obvious question for us is this: To what extent did the scribe really believe that worship at one central shrine, Jerusalem, would support a just society, unlike the imbalanced society of Israel? Perhaps the Deuteronomists believed that it would. If we want to be gracious and put our cynicism aside we might be able to see nothing but the best of intentions in the Deuteronomic movement. If we read the Torah of the Deuteronomist (Deuteronomy, chapters 12 through 26) we will find humanitarian, ethical content. The scribe was supported by the rich and powerful of Jerusalem, those who were in authority. His views were not the same as the views of Amos of Tekoa who saw the structure of a similar society (Israel) as corrupt and unworthy of redemption. Nevertheless, it is a given that the seventh century Deuteronomic movement was greatly influenced by the eighth century prophets, Isaiah, Amos, Hosea, Micah, and others whose oracles have not survived as books of the Bible.

It is possible that Bethel was not an issue in this passage at all. This passage may be a dramatic statement of a basic Deuteronomic issue which can be summed up in these Deuteronomic words of Samuel:

> Has the Lord as great delight in burnt offerings and sacrifices as in obeying?

Here is some information we need. At the time that our scribe was producing his version of the book of Amos, another Torah was being promoted by a group competitive with the Deuteronomists.[3] This competitive Torah, promoted by the Aaronic priesthood (remember that Deuteronomy only speaks of the Levitical priesthood), stressed the ritualistic and ceremonial aspects of Israel's religion. It is this Torah which was later represented by many of the laws typical of the books of Leviticus and Numbers (the P code). The Deuteronomists believed that this Torah of the Aaronic priesthood placed too much emphasis on ceremony and ritual, and it is of this competitive Torah that these words in Jeremiah apply:

> For in the day that I brought them out of the land of Egypt, *I did not speak to your fathers or command them concerning burnt offerings and sacrifices* (italics mine). But this command I gave them, "Obey my voice, and I will be your God and you shall be my people; and walk in all the way that I command you, that it may be well with you" (Jer 7:22–23).

In support of this interpretation we should point out that our scribe wrote, immediately following the words ". . . and righteousness as an ever-flowing stream":

> "Did you bring to me sacrifices and offerings the forty years in the wilderness, O House of Israel . . ." says the LORD, whose name is the God of Hosts (Am 5:25).

Notice that both the passage in Jeremiah (7:22–23) and the editorial insertion in Amos (5:25) support a positive view of the wilderness experience. This positive wilderness experience was a projection into the past of a period when Israel and Yahweh lived together in an ideal relationship without the need of a highly structured ritualistic relationship. The priesthood which competed with the Deuteronomist/Levitical priesthood in the late seventh century did not believe this. The Aaronic priesthood believed that a ritualistic relationship between God and man existed from the beginning of time and was part of the nature of existence. For this reason the observance of the sabbath is firmly rooted in the creation of the world itself (Gen 2:1–3).

It is interesting to note that the school which produced the Torah which competed with the Deuteronomic Torah was, in the following century, successful in reducing the role of the Levites to that of assistants to the Aaronic priests. This school produced the portion of the Tetrateuch which we know as "P." Its role in the development of the Tetrateuch (the first four books of the Bible) enabled this school to place the formation of its Torah chronologically ahead of the D Torah. Eventually both Torahs were recognized by the Jews as all one Torah, and the Penteteuch was recognized as one, unified work, even though it is not.

In the interest of understanding the Bible, however, and in our determination to understand the seventh century version of the book of Amos, it is important to keep these elements in mind.

Our conclusion in this section is that the Deuteronomists were greatly influenced by the ethical and humanitarian teaching of the eighth century prophets, Amos being the prime example. This fact is highlighted for us when we compare the Torah of the Deuteronomist with the Torah of the Aaronic priesthood.

The Final Author

The final author/editor of the book of Amos lived in the sixth century, toward the end of the exile of Judah. When he read the book of Amos he read the seventh century version. The last paragraph contained these words:

> The Lord, God of Hosts,
> he who touches the earth and it melts . . .
> and all who dwell in it mourn,
> and all of it rises like the Nile of Egypt;
> . . . the LORD is his name (Am 9:5–6).

These words about the earth describe for us an earthquake. Perhaps you remember in the first verse of the book:

> The words of Amos . . . which he saw concerning Israel . . . two years before the earthquake (Amos 1:1).

The seventh century edition began and ended with an earthquake. No wonder the people mourned (Am 9:7). Reading the seventh century edition of Amos, it was obvious to the final editor that this book was not complete. Its readers now would need an optimistic ending. And the theology of the day would offer them one.

Let's go back to the beginning. By destroying the rich and powerful of Israel (Samaria), God's anger was mollified, his justice satisfied. So far so good. But what happened to those whom Amos had called the righteous, the many families of rural Israel? What price did they pay for the sins of their oppressors? It would be naive for us to believe that after the ruling elite of Israel were destroyed, somehow the new decision makers would be fair and just. And, like it or not, it is never possible to go back to a better time in the past. It was not possible for Israel to return to a pre-monarchical mode of government where the family (the *beth-av*) had been the central institution of society, the institution around which all other institutions revolved, and the one which was supported by all others. In that idealistic time in the past each family was envisioned as having its own land (passed from generation to generation through the male line) and all things were shared, risks, responsibilities and resources. In the rural areas where Amos lived there had been a community memory of a time when no one class of society oppressed and abused all other classes. It was the disparity between this community memory and the economic reality of the day that accounts for the source of Amos' anger and passion.

At the end of the sixth century there were no more exploiters in Judah, only the exploited. They were tired and weary. They needed something to look forward to. The final editor gave the reader a picture of coming rural prosperity, where one farming activity, harvest, would overtake another, sowing of new seed, and all in an atmosphere of peace and security.

Our message to one another is that God's ultimate purpose is not to punish or destroy, but to give life in beauty and in joy. God's wrath must be balanced with his mercy. Our ultimate hope is a world of justice where everyone will be able to plant vineyards and drink their wine, and make gardens and eat their fruit.

> I will plant them upon their land,
>   and they shall never again be plucked up
>   out of the land which I have given them,
>   says the LORD your God.

Notes

Introduction

1. David Hopkins, *The Highlands of Canaan* (Sheffield: JSPT Press, 1985), p. 56.

I. How Some Scholars Have Divided the Book of Amos

1. We know that Jeremiah had a secretary/scribe who wrote at his direction. For example read Jeremiah 36:27–28.
2. James Luther Mays, *Amos, A Commentary* (Philadelphia: Westminster Press, 1969).
3. Hans Walter Wolff, *Joel and Amos*, trans. Waldemar Janzen et al. (Philadelphia: Fortress Press, 1977).
4. Robert B. Coote, *Amos Among the Prophets* (Philadelphia: Fortress Press, 1981).
5. Mays, *Amos*, p. 12.
6. *Ibid.*, p. vii.
7. Wolff, *Amos*, p. x.
8. *Ibid.*, p. 106.
9. *Ibid.*, p. 108.
10. *Ibid.*, p. 113.
11. *Ibid.*, p. 112.
12. *Ibid.*, p. 113.
13. *Ibid.*
14. Coote, *Amos Among the Prophets*, p. 7.
15. *Ibid.*, p. 11.
16. *Ibid.*, p. 16.
17. *Ibid.*, p. 103.
18. *Ibid.*, pp. 46–109.

19. *Ibid.*, pp. 102–03.
20. *Ibid.*, p. 65.
21. Hans Walter Wolff, *Amos the Prophet*, trans. Foster McCurley (Philadelphia: Fortress Press, 1973).
22. Coote, *Amos*, p. 110.
23. *Ibid.*, p. 124.
24. Robert R. Wilson, *Prophecy and Society in Ancient Israel* (Philadelphia: Fortress Press, 1980), p. 273.

II. Amos, the Eighth Century Prophet of Tekoa

1. Coote, *ibid.*
2. Norman K. Gottwald, *The Tribes of Yahweh* (Maryknoll: Orbis Press, 1979).
3. Gerhard Von Rad, *Old Testament Theology*, Vol. I (New York: Harper and Row, 1962), p. 35.

III. A Sociological Detour

1. Reference here is made to books such as *The Highlands of Canaan* by David Hopkins and *The Tribes of Yahweh* by Norman Gottwald.

IV. The Seventh Century Scribe of Jerusalem

1. Wolff, *Amos and Joel*, p. 112.
2. Robert R. Wilson, *Prophecy and Society in Ancient Israel* (Philadelphia: Westminster Press, 1984).
3. Hans W. Wolff and Walter Brueggemann, *The Vitality of Old Testament Traditions*, "The Kerygma of the Deuteronomic Work" (Altlanta: John Knox Press, 1975), pp. 91–93.
4. Coote, *ibid.*, p. 43.
5. Wilson, *ibid.*
6. Wolff, *Amos the Prophet, The Man and His Background* trans. Foster Mc Curley (Philadelphia: Fortress Press, 1973).

V. The Final Author of the Book of Amos

1. Wolff, *Amos and Joel*, p. 159.
2. For a thorough discussion of the sociology of pre-monarchical Israel, the primary source is Norman Gottwald's book *The Tribes of Yahweh* (Maryknoll: Orbis, 1979). I have written more extensively about this field as it relates to Amos in my dissertation entitled *Preaching from Amos to Address Issues of Economic Injustice*, D. Min., Lancaster Seminary, 1987. Dr. Gottwald's book provided the foundation for my approach.

VII. Spiritual Truth from the Authors of Amos

1. For a discussion of this subject see Walter Brueggemann, *The Prophetic Imagination* (Philadelphia: Fortress Press, 1978).
2. Klaus Koch, *The Prophets, The Assyrian Period* (Philadelphia: Fortress Press, 1983), pp. 53–62.
3. For a thorough discussion of the existence of a Torah which stressed the importance of sacrifices and offerings and was competitive with the Torah of the Deuteronomists, which made its first appearance in the days of Josiah (or shortly following his death), please see *The Exile and Biblical Narrative* by Richard Friedman (Scholars Press, Chico, California, 1981), pp. 69–76.

Postscript: Ten Homiletical Themes from the Book of Amos

1. *The Voice of Pain May Be the Voice of God*

God spoke through Amos who spoke for the poor and the powerless of Israel. Today we must listen to the voice of pain and suffering in our world. It may be the voice of God.

2. *Unwelcome Truth*

They hate him who reproves in the gate (5:10).

Those who speak for God are not always embraced. The message of Amos was not welcome in Samaria or Bethel. Amaziah would not allow him to speak in Bethel and sent him back to Judah. Amos was a skeleton at the feast.

3. *Unacceptable Ritual*

I hate I despise your feast days (5:21ff).

The only ritual which is accepted by God is that which is accompanied by a life of fairness and justice.

4. *The First Shall Be Last*

The rich and powerful of Samaria would be publicly humiliated and marched away to foreign captivity. (The strong shall not retain his strength, nor shall the mighty save his life—Amos 2:14–16. Also see 5:3.)

5. *RSVP*

The scribe of Jerusalem expected a response from his readers. He knew that if his readers would repent and return to

God they would receive his restoring grace. God wants us to respond to his invitation.

6. *What the Prophet Did Not Say*

When we identify the part of the book which belongs to the original prophet, Amos of Tekoa, we find that Amos did not predict the fall of Israel because of idolatry or because the people worshiped false pagan gods. Also, he did not carry words of condemnation because the Israelites mistreated the prophets. He spoke of only one sin: the selfish greed of the rich and powerful of Samaria in preventing the fair distribution of the earth's resources among all the people of Israel. It is when we discover the intensity of the original oracles of Amos that we discover the roots of social justice in the Old Testament.

7. *Making Just Decisions*

Decisions made in Samaria adversely affected the general population of Israel. These decisions favored the royal family, the royal court, the urban merchant class, the professional military establishment, and other vested interests of those located in Samaria. The average citizen of Israel in the days of Amos saw his or her life destroyed economically and was helpless to do anything about it. For justice to rule, all those affected must take part in the decision making process.

8. *God Provides a Voice for Those Who Have No Voice*

Amos spoke on behalf of the rural poor of Israel. God provides a spokesperson for the weak and oppressed. In our own age persons such as Martin Luther King, Caesar Chavez, and Mother Teresa have been the voice of the poor.

9. *False Security*

> Woe unto you who are at ease in Zion
> and to those who feel secure on the mountain of
> Samaria.

The citizens of Samaria felt comfortable and secure, but they were not living a life pleasing to God. A day of judgment was in the near future, so the rich had only a false feeling of security. There is only true security when we are at peace with God.

10. God's Grace Has the Final Word

The book of Amos was not complete until the words of God's restoring love were added by its final author.

Recommended Reading

The books in this list have been selected with the religious professional in mind. These are the persons who are so busy laboring in the world of human need that they simply may not have time to enjoy the luxury of digging into the vast amount of scholarship available. The field of Old Testament scholarship is currently complex, exciting, and expanding. Here are recommendations for the beginning and intermediate Bible student. We can assume that the advanced student has his or her own list of books and articles.

The Total Picture

You cannot understand a book of the Bible in a vacuum. For getting the broad picture *Reading the Old Testament* by Lawrence Boadt (Mahwah: Paulist Press, 1984) gives an excellent picture of the entire Old Testament, using a textbook approach with many helpful maps and charts. Two one-volume Bible commentaries which contain essential articles on Old Testament history, customs, and concepts (along with commentaries for each book of the Bible, including Amos) are *The Jerome Bible Commentary* (Prentice-Hall, 1968) and *The Interpreter's Bible* (Nashville: Abingdon, 1971).

The Book of Amos

In addition to the three books on Amos mentioned in Chapter I (by Mays, Wolff, and Coote) these are interesting: Wolff, in an earlier book, tries to establish *clan wisdom* as the environment from which Amos' oracles grew (Philadelphia: Fortress, 1973). For an archaeological perspective read *Amos, Hosea, Micah—An Archaeological Commentary* by Philip J. King (Philadelphia: Westminster, 1987). King's findings concerning Amos also appear as an article in *Biblical Archaeology Review*, entitled "The Marzeah Amos Denounces," Vol. XV No. 4, July/August 1988. A new book entitled *Amos, the Eighth-Century Prophet* by John H. Hayes presents a view opposed to the view offered in this book. Dr. Hayes says that the 8th century prophet wrote most of the book of Amos. (Nashville: Abingdon Press). There is a book devoted to chapters 1 and 2 of Amos, *Amos's Oracles Against the Nations* by John Barton (Cambridge: Cambridge University Press, 1980). For an approach to a book of prophecy similar in approach to this book see *Micah, A Commentary* by J.L. Mays (Philadelphia: Westminster, 1976). A small book, easy to understand, is *Studying the Book of Amos* by John D.W. Watts (Nashville: Broadman Press, 1966).

Other Related Subjects

Sections in the one-volume Bible commentaries mentioned above on the Deuteronomic school and the Deuteronomistic history should be read. Another slim volume on this subject is *Joshua, Judges, Samuel, Kings* by W.E. Rast (Philadelphia: Fortress Press, 1978). For the intermediate student two books by J. Blenkinsopp are recommended, *Prophecy and Canon* (Notre Dame: University of Notre Dame Press, 1977) and *A History of Prophecy in Israel* (Philadelphia: Westminster, 1983). For an excellent sociological approach to life in ancient Israel I recommend Part VI (pp. 237–343) entitled "Models of the Social Structure: All Israel; Protective Associations; Extended Families," in *The Tribes of Yahweh* by Norman Gottwald (Maryknoll: Orbis Books, 1979). I also recommend David Hopkins' book *The Highlands of Canaan*, especially chapter IX, "Agricultural Objectives and Strategies: Risk Spreading and the Optimization of Labor," and chapter X, "Subsistence Challenges and the Emergence of Israel."

Finally, for an exposition of the hypothesis concerning the existence of two competing Torahs at the end of the seventh century, consult *The Exile and Biblical Narrative* by Richard Friedman (Chico: Scholars Press, 1981).